KAUTO STAR
& DENMAN

KAUTO STAR
& DENMAN

The Epic Story of Two Champions
Who Set the Racing World on Fire

JONATHAN POWELL

WEIDENFELD & NICOLSON

First published in Great Britain in 2010
by Weidenfeld & Nicolson

1 3 5 7 9 10 8 6 4 2

A CIP catalogue record for this book is available from the British Library.

ISBN: 978 0 297 86312 0

Printed in Great Britain by Butler Tanner & Dennis Ltd

The Orion Publishing Group's policy is to use papers that are natural,
renewable and recyclable and made from wood grown in sustainable forests.
The logging and manufacturing processes are expected to conform to
environmental regulations of the country of origin.

Weidenfeld & Nicolson

Orion Publishing Group Ltd
Orion House
5 Upper Saint Martin's Lane
London, WC2H 9EA

An Hachette UK Company

www.orionbooks.co.uk

This book is dedicated to the
memory of my mother Doreen Powell
who supported my choice of a career
in racing journalism when it seemed a distant,
elusive dream and backed me all the way.

Jonathan Powell. June, 2010.

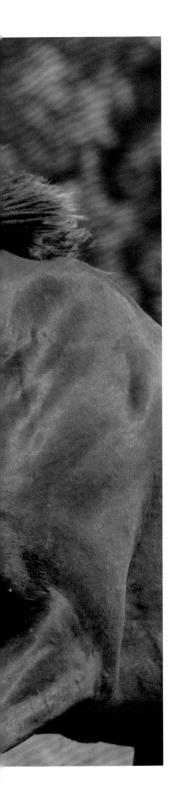

ACKNOWLEDGEMENTS

I could not have attempted to write this book without the generous co-operation of Paul Nicholls and so many of his staff. To be able to frequently visit a busy training yard housing so many exceptional horses has been a considerable bonus for which I am extremely grateful. To spend time at Manor Farm Stables is to appreciate that Paul's skill at running a happy ship is at the core of his unrelenting success. My thanks in particular go to Clifford Baker, Dan Skelton, Sarah West, Donna Blake and Robert Baker for patiently answering so many questions. My thanks also to Sonia Warburton, Nick Child, Jess Allen and Lucinda Gould, the quartet who have looked after the two chasers at the heart of this book. Their countless long hours of hard work have been rewarded with an astonishing ride to the highest peaks of steeplechasing. The jockeys who have ridden Kauto Star and Denman have given fascinating insights about them. My thanks to Jerome Guiheneuf, Ruby Walsh, Christian Williams, Sam Thomas and Tony McCoy for reliving so many outstanding moments... and a few less happy ones.

Researching the early days of the two horses was a delight. Henri Aubert and Serge Foucher proved to be a fund of information on Kauto Star with Liz Price acting as the most skilful of interpreters. Anthony Bromley and David Powell then provided key details of the tricky, drawn out negotiations, which eventually saw Kauto Star arrive at Ditcheat. Colman O'Flynn, Edmond Kent and my old friend Adrian Maguire recalled with vivid detail the formative years of Denman and Denis Buckley provided early photographs of the youngster who would turn into a monster.

I also appreciate the help of Clive Smith, Paul & Marianne Barber and Harry Findlay who have played a considerable part in this book. To listen to Harry in full flow about his punting activities was an education.

I would also like to thank Tim Cox and Danny Molony for providing background detail, Pip Pocock and my daughters Tara and Lydia for their assistance as eagle-eyed proof-readers, and Richard Pickford and his staff for their technical assistance. My greatest thanks, though, go to Paul Nicholls who has given me unprecedented access to the two horses he has trained with a master's touch and those closest to them. Without his whole-hearted support this project would have been left at the start.

CONTENTS

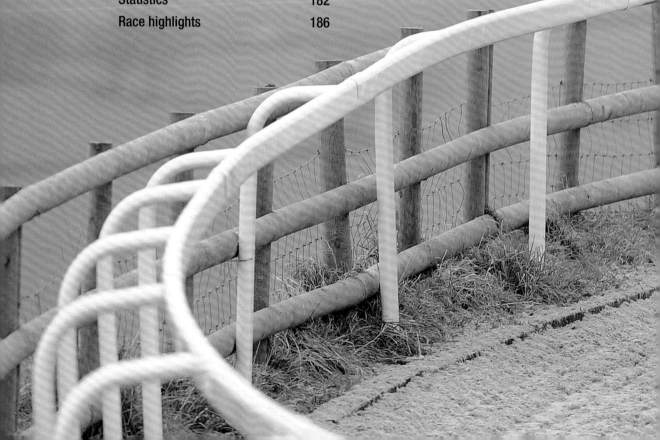

CHAPTER 1

NEIGHBOURS

Showdowns in sport have rarely promised more than the clash between two giants of steeplechasing in a special corner of the Cotswolds in the 2010 Tote Cheltenham Gold Cup. So many present at the course had invested their hopes, their dreams and their hard cash on the outcome of the seismic encounter between horses stabled next to each other at the Somerset yard of their trainer Paul Nicholls.

In the champion's corner stood the handsome bay Kauto Star, indisputably the finest chaser for many years. He was trying to win the race for the third time on his tenth birthday and would be ridden, as usual, by the brilliantly gifted Irishman Ruby Walsh and was overwhelmingly the favourite in the ring at odds of 8-11.

In the challenger's corner, pawing the ground with impatience, was his neighbour Denman, a no-nonsense, tungsten-tough liver chestnut who had stolen the crown from his stable-mate in 2008 with a ruthlessly efficient display of jumping and stamina. The presence of the record-breaking champion jockey Tony McCoy on his back added further spice to a duel which was widely seen as the decider since the score between them was 1–1 in the race that matters most in the jumping calendar. This time Denman was a solid second favourite at 4-1.

Their clash dominated the headlines and the betting to the exclusion of all others in the super-charged build-up to the most widely anticipated Gold Cup for years. No one could doubt that they deserved to share top billing ahead of a mouth-watering collision of racing values. We had the poetry of the sleekly gifted, French-bred champion matched against the raw clinical power of a relentless battleship who, at times, can behave like a member of the awkward squad.

You could argue that at times the scale of the non-stop promotion of the clash of the titans was guilty of ignoring the other players. The Tote's battle bus, emblazoned with massive photos of both horses, travelled for weeks from town to town, much like a circus on tour. It was uncannily similar to the madness of the last week of a general election when the leaders of the biggest political parties criss-cross the country at breakneck speed seeking our support.

Denman and Kauto Star side by side in their boxes at Ditcheat.

At the same time big-screen action on the four days of the festival featured the brutal exchanges between Nigel Benn and Chris Eubank as they fought ferociously for the WBO middleweight title twenty years ago. Benn and Eubank. Coe v Ovett. Grundy and Bustino. Senna v Prost. Borg and McEnroe. Even Rangers v Celtic. The message was unmistakable as some of the most compelling sporting duels of the past were trotted out in print and on television ahead of the Gold Cup.

As the publicity machine moved into overdrive Cheltenham upped the ante by selling scarves and badges to supporters of Kauto Star and Denman. The demand was so strong that 6,000 had been snapped up by the big day. For the record the split was 61% in favour of Kauto Star. Other merchandise on offer included hats, rosettes and bracelets in the colours of the two horses. In addition celebrities with an interest in racing were invited to deliver their verdicts on the showdown. Jodie Kidd, Frankie Dettori and Jeremy Kyle were among those favouring Kauto Star while Michael Owen was firmly in the Denman camp.

David Haye, the world champion heavyweight boxer, took things to a new level by appearing at Ditcheat in a series of promotional photographs with the two protagonists. Haye's thoughts on the forthcoming confrontation were hardly original as he suggested that the Gold Cup was racing's own version of the 'Rumble in the Jungle' between Mohammed Ali and George Foreman. But you couldn't argue with his view that Kauto Star was brilliantly talented and flashy like Ali while Denman was a slugger in the style of Foreman.

Naturally Paul Nicholls, the trainer of Kauto Star and Denman, played his part. Should he ever decide to turn away from racing he could make a fortune in public relations. Trainers from a different era used to scatter man traps beside the gallops to discourage visitors and lock up their lads at night to prevent word of impressive work-outs reaching the ears of punters. How times have changed.

Nicholls cannot be faulted in his desire to keep the public informed at every turn. He appreciates the ever-increasing demands of the media, tries to help whenever he can and answers every question frankly. Late in February he paraded his Cheltenham squad before a media scrum that stretched well into three figures. Nicholls posed for endless photos with his own two imposing heavyweights, then chatted at length with dozens of journalists before giving one-to-one interviews with more than twenty TV and radio crews.

World heavyweight champion boxer David Haye poses with two other champions, soon to slug it out at Cheltenham in the 2010 Gold Cup.

Nigel Twiston-Davies observed the undeniably one-sided Gold Cup build-up with ill-disguised irritation from his wind-swept eyrie at Naunton on the roof of the Cotswolds a dozen miles from Cheltenham where he was preparing his course specialist Imperial Commander to dismantle Kauto Star and Denman. A genial, down-to-earth countryman with a ready smile and a passion for steeplechasing, he plays the role of the shy, retiring racehorse trainer with a master's touch. Perhaps he learned at the knee of Greta Garbo. After Earth Summit won the Grand National for him in 1998 he famously left that old BBC smoothie Des Lynam speechless as he told him, "I don't do interviews"!

It is only fair to point out that Twiston-Davies's sense of PR has improved markedly since that embarrassing comment. Truth be told, conversations with him tend to be highly entertaining since he is an independent spirit with a colourful turn of phrase and prefers to state things as he sees them. In March 2010 he was certainly irked that most professional observers were ignoring the legitimate claims of Imperial Commander in the clamour to salute the pair who headed the market.

"It was difficult hearing about those other two all the time because I thought we were going to win it," he said with feeling. His belief in the ex

Overleaf: Working out on the gallops.

Irish point-to-pointer Imperial Commander had been unshakeable since he all but lowered the colours of Kauto Star in a compelling finish to the Betfair Chase at Haydock in November 2009. The verdict? A nose.

"From every angle I thought we'd got it. Only the judge thought we'd lost that one but Imperial Commander finished so well I felt if there had been another two furlongs he'd have won by miles. Afterwards we seemed to be forgotten," he suggested, more in surprise than anger.

It was not entirely by coincidence that Twiston-Davies seemed to slip under the radar in the run-up to Cheltenham because, given the choice, he still prefers to shun the limelight. Yet part of the appeal of racing is its unfailing capacity to turn conventional wisdom on its head, and the improbable result of the 2010 Gold Cup ensured that no one would be ignoring Nigel Twiston-Davies in the months that followed.

When the talking was finally over on Friday 19th March, we were given an early reminder that sport doesn't allow you to parade past achievements and doesn't stop asking for more. Soon after the tapes rose we discovered that there were three prize-fighters in the ring and eventually found ourselves marvelling at the sight of Imperial Commander appearing like a winged assassin to outrun Denman and lift the crown in a thunderous conclusion to an astonishingly tense race.

Kauto Star, normally so sure-footed, crashed out heavily at the fourth last fence, mercifully without injury, while Denman, though staying on with admirable resolution, was unable to resist the spring-heeled Commander in the closing stages. We suspected that we had witnessed a crucial changing of the guard, though euphoria has long been the enemy of judgement and the harrowing sight of the best chaser of modern times on the ground raised legitimate questions about the true value of the winner's performance.

For the moment, however, Imperial Commander reigned supreme. His triumphant charge was without blemish – controlled, measured and full of courage – although we would soon be given a harsh reminder of just how hard it is to keep a champion at his peak. In the Totesport Bowl at Aintree, twenty days after the Gold Cup, chasing's new hero came tumbling down to earth with an abject display of jumping before unseating Paddy Brennan at the fourteenth fence with one blunder too many.

Denman and Kauto Star have long shown that the real merit is not just in winning status but retaining it. No one can deny that they have already earned their place in steeplechasing's hall of fame. This is their story.

Left to right: Harry Findlay, Paul Barber, Denman, Paul Nicholls, Kauto Star and Clive Smith.

Round 3 in the Cheltenham Gold Cup ... Clive Smith and Harry Findlay defend their corners.

CHAPTER 2

L'EXTRATERRESTRE

The two horses that would change the landscape of jump racing were born less than a month apart in the spring of the new Millennium. First to arrive early on 19 March in the picturesque village of Le Lion d'Angers in the Loire valley was a bonny bay colt, soon to be named Kauto Star. The birth of Kauto Relka's third foal would in time become an event of national importance to the locals.

Kauto Relka belonged to Henri Aubert, a short, stocky, twinkle-eyed stockman who began his breeding enterprise in 1977 while driving machinery and delivering merchandise for a farm co-operative. The son of a farmer with a handful of acres, he shared his parents' interest in racing and longed for the day when he would have the chance to breed his own horses. It came in the mid-seventies when he fell for the charms of a modest mare, Verdurette, who was prevented from racing any further at five because she had won insufficient prize money on the flat.

He recalls "I was taken to inspect her at the stables of her trainer Edmond Boulanger by a friend who knew I was interested in breeding. I saw three others that day but kept coming back to Verdurette. Why? To me, anyway, she looked really good. I thought she was beautiful and she was by Lionel. So it wasn't a bad family."

Aubert paid around 700 Euros for Verdurette. Her first foal, named Un d'Avril because he was born on 1 April 1978, won seven times. A second foal, Kautovent, was placed eleven times in fourteen starts. Aubert was in the foothills of his life as a thoroughbred breeder. Finances were tight and initially he kept his breeding stock at his father-in-law's farm near by at Nyoiseau, but an equine lottery was about to set in motion an improbable sequence of events that would seal his place in jumping folklore.

Kauto Relka, Kauto Star's dam, with foal in 2005.

Most years the National Stud invited breeders to enter a ballot for a free covering by one of their stallions. In 1980 Aubert's name came out first in the draw. He celebrated his good fortune by sending Verdurette to Kautokeino at the National Stud. It was a sound choice. Kautokeino was a stallion in demand, and in normal circumstances would have been beyond Aubert's price range. The result of the mating was Kautorette, who would prove to be the foundation mare of his stud and become the granddam of Kauto Star. There was an unfortunate sequel to the story when Verdurette died a month after foaling. After an urgent search failed to identify a suitable foster mother in the area Henri Aubert raised the orphan foal with bottles of milk.

"Luckily my wife helped out. Every two hours one of us would feed the filly. That's how it was. She was not as cheeky as the others, not as forward but she progressed very pleasingly," he relates. The countless extra hours spent by the Auberts nurturing Kautorette were rewarded when she won eleven races on

The best of friends... Henri Aubert with his great brood mare, Kauto Relka, dam of Kauto Star.

the flat and was placed many more times before returning to his stud after being covered by a stallion at the National Stud. She proved to be barren that first year, so was put back into training and won two minor races over hurdles before tendon problems ended her racing career.

Kautorette bred four individual winners for Henri Aubert, but it was one that did not race who would produce the finest chaser of modern times. Kauto Relka was the result of a mating between Kautorette and the French stallion Port Etienne. Although she was a fine-looking foal, knee problems prevented her from racing, so she stayed at home to continue the family line. In the years ahead Kauto Relka would prove to be a prolific brood mare. Her third offspring by Village Star all but broke the mould.

Village Star was a top-class horse on the flat, good enough to win the Grand Prix de Saint-Cloud as a five year old before finishing fifth in Tony Bin's Prix de l'Arc de Triomphe at Longchamp in 1988. Soon he began a sultan's life at Haras du Grand Chesnaie in Mesnil, sixteen kilometres from Le Lion d'Angers.

"I think the fee was about 600 Euros, so it wasn't too expensive. At that time we could afford stallion fees. Today it is tougher. Village Star's form was top class and I liked him because he was a chestnut," recalls Aubert.

"Kauto Star's birth was extraordinary because it happened so quickly on the evening of 19 March. At 7.30 Kauto Relka started giving birth, and then he was there. I had gone to a reception before and was dressed in my Sunday clothes with a tie. The birth happened perfectly and the foal seemed strong the moment he was born. He had hardly left his mother's belly before he was standing up. I had never seen that before. It was amazing. He just put his hind legs up, then pushed and that was it. From the start he was a special foal, very good looking with a bit of character. He liked to give little kicks or lay his ears back when you put your hand on his back, but it didn't last long."

As a commercial breeder Henri Aubert has tended to keep the fillies and sell the colts. In October, after racing at Lion d'Angers he invited an old friend, the trainer Serge Foucher, to see his horses on the way home. Aubert had once worked for Foucher's father. A year earlier Serge Foucher had bought Kauto Star's half sister, Kauto Lumen Dei, who would go on to win on the flat and over hurdles and fences before her life was cut short by an aneurysm. Now he was keen to discover what else her breeder had to offer. On this particular shopping trip his eye was constantly taken by a jaunty bay colt with a distinctive white blaze on his forehead.

Foucher recalls, "There were five or six foals in a field but I immediately fell in love with Kauto Star. He really stood apart. There was him … and then the others. Oh yes, I took to him straight away. He was the only one I wanted to buy. He was like a giraffe, doing one stride when the others were doing four. He was very big and he was always in front as they dashed round the field. Although he didn't have the best pedigree he was the only one I liked."

To Aubert's dismay the fields 500 metres from his home where he raised Kauto Star and dozens of other foals for eighteen years at Le Lion d'Angers will soon be covered by houses. The nine hectares of rented land were taken back by the local community in May this year. Aubert concedes, "It is a shame it has come to this. I am forced to stop my breeding activity because they will build some houses here. We are proud we have bred a horse like Kauto Star. We only had three mares then and to produce a great champion is something special, no?"

There has been a tangible reward in the shape of regular cheques from breeders' premiums earned by Kauto Star's vast accumulation of glory. Aubert reflects, "Kauto Star changed our life; that cannot be denied. The stallion fee for Village Star certainly paid off and the money we have received has paved some fresh routes for us, but I can tell you I am still the same person and still have the same friends. For me travelling is going to a racetrack. I have been to Cheltenham twice to see Kauto Star win his first Gold Cup and when he finished second a year later."

Kauto Relka was put down in September 2009 at the age of eighteen after injuring her spine while turned out in a paddock. Aubert is grateful to have been involved with such an outstanding mare. "It was a shame it ended like that but I was very lucky with her because she gave me thirteen foals in fourteen years. It has been a dream ride, most of all with Kauto Star. Now her younger offspring are coming through and Kauto Stone, her ninth foal, is maintaining the family reputation," he says.

Kauto Star's first trainer, Serge Foucher, talks movingly about his involvement with the horse who would captivate racegoers on both sides of the Channel. "He was the naughtiest as well as the best horse I've had anything to do with. I've been involved with horses since I was fourteen and been

Kauto Star after winning the Grade 3 Prix de Longchamp at Auteuil in May 2004 with jockey Jerome Guiheneuf and trainer Serge Foucher.

training for almost thirty years, but none has compared with Kauto Star," he says.

"I felt like his father at times. I bought him when he was just six months old and brought him up. From very early on he had an extraordinary character. He already seemed like an adult when he was still a foal. He was very nasty, too, much stronger than the others of the same age. When he arrived you couldn't go into his box, he was that nasty, showing far too much character. In all my time as a trainer he was the first one I have seen like that.

"We really had a lot of trouble with him so we gelded him straight away before breaking him in. His testicles at just over six months were already the size you would expect to find on a two year old. He was a real male, rejected food from the trough while others were around and would only eat if he was by himself. He was also domineering, forever trying to bite and kick other horses, and we had to sedate him every time we clipped his coat.

"We had problems breaking him in, too, because he was so fragile and unsure. We kept him on the lunge with a saddle for a month and had a really tough time with him because he pulled like mad. We also put a blanket on him to get him used to carrying something on his back and tied him to a wall to try to restrain him. You couldn't make any movement because he was afraid of anything. He certainly had a lot of character."

Foucher usually has around twenty-five horses at his stables at Senonnes, the biggest training centre in the West of France, with upwards of twenty training yards close to the town's racecourse. It was soon apparent that he had a prodigy on his hands.

He relates: "When Kauto Star was only eighteen months old I was already saying that I had a star in my stable. And at two I continued to think it and say it. Already he was impossible, though we had the same guy riding him every day. Then at the end of the two-year-old season we started schooling him in the mornings, and by September he was jumping twice a week, though he didn't respect the smaller fences. He was remarkable while at the same time too confident, tall and awkward, but he learned quickly."

Once Kauto Star began working on the gallops Foucher saw a glimpse of the future that encouraged him to dub the horse l'Extraterrestre. The sight of the youngster dashing past a line of older horses is firmly etched in the trainer's memory.

"He was doing a routine canter as a two year old behind older horses, the lead horses, but the rider couldn't hold him any longer and let him overtake all the others. I knew immediately that he was a very good horse, in a class of his own. He was so fast he was really an aeroplane. I don't run my horses on the flat and he wasn't a flat horse but had he run at two he would have won. No question.

"In the mornings he was always impressive, maybe even more impressive than when he began racing. At Senonnes we had never seen a horse like him. When he was two a potential buyer came to see him, but Kauto Star kicked the poor fellow in the head. I thought he was dead when I saw him lying on the floor, but thankfully he recovered. At least Kauto Star got away with not being sold."

Most Irish-bred jump horses are not seen on a racecourse until they are four or five years old. French-breds tend to be more precocious. That was certainly the case with Kauto Star, who was sufficiently forward for Foucher to run him in the first three-year-old hurdle of the year over 2,900 metres at Bordeaux Le Bouscat on 1 March 2003, almost a month short of his third birthday.

It was a race laced with controversy. Kauto Star, ridden by Fabrice Barrao, made a winning début by a short head from his stable companion Star Glory despite veering across the track in the closing stages. An objection by the runner-up's jockey Christophe Pieux was thrown out, but his subsequent appeal led to the result being reversed. In a long-winded explanation the stewards concluded that the narrow winner had hung persistently across the course on the run in, taking Star Glory with him.

The promise shown by Kauto Star attracted immediate interest. Shortly before the horse claimed his first success at Enghien in April on his second start Foucher sold third shares to Claude Cohen and Claude Lellouche while retaining the remaining 33% for himself and his wife. Two more victories followed at Auteuil. Already a pattern was emerging of a vibrant talent allied to a pleasing willingness to fight hard at the finish.

Foucher relates: "He had a temperament of steel, an extraordinary temperament. He always ate up, never left anything, and the day after a race you wouldn't have known he had run. He would walk like a Seigneur. In the mornings I knew I had a champion. Yet he was not a strong horse, not a bulldozer, more a giraffe."

Kauto Star's eye-catching sequence of victories was halted by a fall at Auteuil in October when he was ridden for the second time by Foucher's new stable jockey Jerome Guiheneuf who recalls "He fell because the going was very heavy. He went for a big jump and couldn't recover in the ground. It wasn't so much a mistake, just a lack of experience."

The race was won by the brilliantly gifted filly, Maia Eria. Later that season she would overwhelm Kauto Star three more times, twice by the comprehensive margin of nineteen lengths. Had racegoers already seen the best of him? Guiheneuf puts those defeats down to a bout of sickness while the horse was stabled at Pau at the foot of the Pyrenees close to the Spanish border. He explains, "He became ill while at Pau for regular schooling over the big steeplechase fences. There was a bug going around at the time and he got it. He had flu or something and was ill for a month and a half. So we took it easy with him. In his next three races he was second, fifth and third. Then he recovered and began to progress gently."

Whatever the reason, Kauto Star was transformed when he appeared in a valuable Grade 3 Hurdle at Auteuil on 30 May 2004. Five weeks earlier he had finished a weary third, far behind Maia Eria. This time he bounced back to form at the rewarding odds of 36-1 with the easiest possible success by eight lengths from River Charm, with Maia Eria out of the money.

While acknowledging that the horse had been sick Foucher believes the startling improvement in form was chiefly down to new tactics. He says, "What happened was simple. I like my horses to run from the front, so Jerome always went to take the lead on Kauto Star and made the running for the others. He did it a few times on the horse and I thought it wasn't suiting him. This time I suggested he be more patient. So he rode him in fourth or fifth position and won easily."

Guiheneuf will never forget the raw power of Kauto Star that day. "He felt like a champion, no question, and I had no doubt he was the best I have ever ridden. I don't think there will be another like him," he declares. Already the jockey was anticipating a long, rewarding association with a horse who offered untold promise. His dreams were about to be rudely shattered.

The man who would spirit Kauto Star away from France arrived out of the blue at Paul Nicholls' yard on a Sunday morning in August 2003. Clive Smith, an accountant, is a golfing nut who bought his first set of clubs with his earnings during the time he worked briefly as a caddy during the school holidays and was soon paying three shillings and sixpence to play a round of golf inside Ascot racecourse.

"I was lucky enough to play at some decent courses but couldn't work out where the ordinary guy liked to play. So I set out to build one for them to pay and play," he recounts.

He advertised for a site, leased a farm in Surrey and raised the funds by selling his house, his car and some shares, then borrowed as much money as he could from his bank manager, a fellow member of Camberley Golf Club. "I was so focused I had time for nothing else," he recalls. "If it hadn't worked out I'd probably have ended up with nothing. As I didn't even have a clubhouse I settled for an old caravan, which cost £100 plus £30 for delivery. I just had to last out the two years I spent building the course without ending up bankrupt."

He mowed the greens, dug out the bunkers, and regularly took his turn behind the counter in the caravan when the course opened in May 1978. The sheer number of golfers pouring through the door from the start indicated that he had backed a sure-fire winner. He then struck pure gold with his second course, Hawthorn Hill, once the home of pony racing, which he later sold on for £8 million and then built a third course.

Smith had been intrigued by racing since his first early experience as a small boy at Royal Ascot in 1950. He walked the three miles from his home to the course with his mother and brother and remembers watching spellbound

Overleaf: The sight which captivated Clive Smith. Kauto Star is majestic in triumph at Auteuil in May, 2004.

27

from the infield as Doug Smith came from last to first to win the Gold Cup on Supertello. It left a lasting impression.

"I loved the colour, the pageantry, the characters and the glamour of it all. I thought it was so exciting, a terrific kind of entertainment," he recalls. "Who knows, if I hadn't gone into golf maybe life would have taken a different turn. I think I might even have ended up as a racehorse trainer. It's a business I really think I'd enjoy – the detailed planning, the buzz."

Funds raised from his golfing enterprises eventually allowed Smith the chance to try his luck at racing as an owner. "My first visit to Cheltenham was for the Gold Cup in 1974, the day the favourite Pendil was brought down by High Ken, and I was at Kempton when Arkle was beaten by Dormant in the King George V1 Chase. I can remember reaching out and tapping him on the back as he was led away. Unfortunately he injured a leg that day and never ran again. Now I was ready to try my hand as an owner. I was not going to throw away my money, just buy one horse to see how I liked it," he explains.

Smith's first horse, Hawthorn Hill Lad, proved to be a smart hurdler and he then enjoyed a measure of success as an owner with Jenny Pitman, David Elsworth and later Martin Pipe who trained Royal Auclair to win the Cathcart Chase for him at Cheltenham in 2002, but it was a chance visit to Nicholls yard that pitchforked him into the limelight as an owner.

"The yard was deserted at the time I arrived. When I called out Paul popped his head out of the window of his office upstairs. I introduced myself, told him I had horses with Martin Pipe and was looking for a change. With that he was down the stairs like a shot and came out to greet me," he recounts.

At the time Paul Nicholls was the most go-ahead young jumps trainer in the country. Those who had paid attention to his obvious talent, his work ethic and his appetite for improvement had long forecast that he would be champion trainer sooner rather than later. For the past five seasons, to his evident frustration, he had finished runner-up in the title race to all-conquering Pipe.

Try as he might Nicholls couldn't quite summon the firepower to topple Pipe from his lofty perch, and increasingly the battle for supremacy between the pair was becoming personal. When push came to shove at the end of each season the sheer numbers of horses the champion could call on proved decisive. The two men had emerged from vastly different backgrounds. Nobody should doubt the intensity of purpose that Pipe brought to the task of turning out record numbers of winners from his yard close to the M5, though he was hugely helped in the task by his late father, Dave, the canniest of bookmakers, who invested millions in the project after selling his portfolio of betting shops.

For all his astonishing achievements before his sudden retirement in April 2006, Martin Pipe remained essentially a private man, suspicious of the media. When it came to the running plans of his horses he tended to keep his cards closer to his chest than a magician disguising a favourite trick. Nicholls, in contrast, is an open book in his desire to keep the public informed at every step.

The son of a rugby-playing policeman, Nicholls was set on training racehorses from a remarkably early age. He learned to ride on ponies kept by his father, Brian, in rented stables close to the police house where the family lived near Bristol before enthusiastically working all hours as a lad in the yard of point-to-point legend Dick Baimbridge. Tall and heavily built, he progressed to ride over 100 winners as a professional jockey before a serious leg injury forced him to concede defeat in his long-running battle with the scales.

When Paul Barber advertised his yard for rent in May, 1991 Nicholls proved to be in a different league to the other candidates he interviewed. Barber has never had cause to regret his decision to choose the confident youngster whose enthusiasm, determination and self-belief convinced him that he possessed the qualities to make a success as a trainer. No matter that, at first, he had could muster only eight horses.

Barber recalls: "From the moment Paul arrived for his interview he left us in no doubt about his big ambition to succeed. We liked the fact that he was young and keen because we were looking for someone who would eat, sleep and drink horses. It was immediately apparent that he was not remotely interested in anything else. He was straight-forward, decisive, hard working and promised to fill the stable within the year."

Nicholls rewarded Barber's faith in him in double-quick time. Engagingly positive and outgoing, he swiftly proved to be a trainer who equips the team that works for him with a depth of conviction and strength of organisation from which success inevitably flowed. As the initial trickle of winners from Ditcheat turned into a flood he was forced to add more boxes each summer to accommodate the conveyor belt of horses arriving from an ever-increasing band of wealthy owners drawn to a trainer who was clearly heading for the top.

The first meeting between Clive Smith and Paul Nicholls on that summer's morning in 2003 was to have a huge impact on jump racing. Like so many visitors to Manor Farm stables, Smith was immediately impressed by the ambitious young trainer and his facilities. Within days he had transferred Royal Auclair and Rainbow Frontier from Pipe to Nicholls and hinted more than once that he was ready to make a major investment.

He explains, "I was looking to get more seriously involved, to increase my numbers of horses, and wanted a trainer who would be relaxed, open and friendly with me. I liked what I'd seen of Paul on television and after a very short time with him I knew he was the right person."

Rainbow Frontier, invariably unsound, was swiftly retired but Royal Auclair, despite the hint of a wind problem, ended a rewarding season for owner and trainer by finishing a close second in the Betfred Gold Cup at Sandown late in April 2004. Smith felt it was time to up the ante.

"I was in my early sixties and decided to put aside £1 million to spend on racing as a fun investment. I was single, the business was going well and I had a bit of spare money, so why not? I wasn't into yachts or anything," he says.

Nicholls trained an outstanding young chasing prospect, Garde Champetre, who was due to go through the sales ring at Doncaster in May as his owners, the Million in Mind partnership, sell their horses at the end of each season. Nicholls was mad keen to keep the horse and quickly persuaded Smith to try to buy him, though on the day he was many miles away at Gogmagog golf course hosting the final of the Lagonda Trophy, a golf event he sponsors each year for promising amateurs which has been won by such illustrious names as Lee Westwood and Luke Donald.

So Nicholls took charge at Doncaster, where the market for jump horses was exceptionally strong. Nothing that passed through the ring was more popular than Garde Champetre. Initially Nicholls hoped to buy him for around 400,000 guineas but that was soon exposed as a highly optimistic estimate. The price soared swiftly during several minutes of frantic bidding until Nicholls' last throw at 490,000 guineas. It was not enough.

Moments later, Garde Champetre was knocked down to J. P. McManus, who at the time was part owner of Manchester United, for 530,000 guineas, a world record price at auction for a National Hunt horse. Initially Smith and Nicholls were dismayed, but in time they would appreciate that they had enjoyed a great escape. Garde Champetre was injured that summer and never fulfilled his enormous promise, though late in his career he enjoyed a fine revival in cross-country chases.

The search for a suitable recruit for Clive Smith immediately moved to France. Five years previously, wary of being asked to pay exorbitant prices in

Ireland, Nicholls had begun to switch the emphasis of his recruiting policy across the Channel where jump horses tend to be more forward and less costly. He was helped in this task by an eager young bloodstock agent, Anthony Bromley, joint partner with David Minton in Highflyer Bloodstock. Bromley readily admits that his initial foray for Nicholls in France was not particularly productive, but he had a useful network of contacts there, had previously found a number of useful horses for Nicky Henderson and was impressively quick to strike once a horse came on the market.

For almost a year Bromley had been monitoring the exploits of Kauto Star. He'd seen videos of some of his victories as a three year old, but hadn't been tempted at first because he wasn't qualified for races like the Triumph Hurdle since he was no longer a novice. Kauto Star had also come off second best every time he met Maia Eria.

Bromley noted a significant drop in Kauto Star's form and was then stunned by the manner of his victory at Auteuil on the Sunday following the Doncaster Sales. He watched the race in his office at Newmarket, took the precaution of taping it and wondered if Foucher could be persuaded to part company with Kauto Star. Six days later Bromley was due at Epsom to see Gatwick, a horse he had bought as a yearling, run in the Derby. The suspicion that he might be able to set up a deal to buy Kauto Star led to an urgent change of plan.

He relates "I was blown away by the sight of Kauto Star winning at Auteuil so easily at long odds and loved the way he saw off Maia Eria who had regularly thumped him that season. This big turn round in form suggested Kauto Star had improved out of all knowledge. At first I didn't think he'd be for sale because his trainer Serge Foucher, who owned a share in him, was dead against it. In addition Serge was not normally a seller".

The day after the race Bromley's French based scout David Powell called to say that one of Kauto Star's owners Claude Lellouche had made it known that a substantial bid had already been received for the horse from another agent. Despite the continuing opposition of the trainer he was on the market at the right price. Powell immediately began lengthy negotiations with Foucher. Bromley had already arranged for video tapes of Kauto Star's latest race to be couriered to Clive Smith and Paul Nicholls. Aware that he had to act fast or someone else would beat them in the rush to buy the horse, Bromley then tabled an offer on the Wednesday and a deal was agreed the following day. All that remained, it seemed, was to complete the formality of a veterinary inspection. But nothing in this transaction would be straightforward.

Overleaf: A study of elegance... Kauto Star.

Bromley takes up the story "We'd just missed out on Garde Champetre and we didn't want to fail again so it made sense for me to go to France on Derby day with Paul's vet Buffy Shirley-Beavan. I thought there might be problems because the trainer was reluctant to sell. It was shaping up to be the most expensive purchase of my career and I didn't want any last minute hitches if things became a bit tricky."

He continues "We were concerned about the reception that Buffy might get and took David Powell along in case we needed an interpreter. Sure enough when we arrived at Serge Foucher's yard it was obvious he was still against selling Kauto Star, though he was perfectly pleasant. He did say the horse had been sick in midwinter and had not been spot on when he raced in the early spring. Then, apparently, he blossomed before his eye-catching victory at Auteuil when his old rival Maia Eria was only fifth."

Bromley and Shirley-Beavan watched the horse on the gallops, ridden by his regular jockey Jerome Guiheneuf, but Foucher had vanished by the time the vet needed to perform the essential task of scoping Kauto Star to check his larynx and see if he bled internally. The horse then resolutely refused to allow the vet to thread the scoping tube up his nostrils. The only option left was to sedate him to allow the vet to pass the endoscope up his nose, but that couldn't be done without the permission of the trainer and he was nowhere to be seen.

Bromley recalls, "We realised that Serge had disappeared into the French countryside shortly after we returned from the gallops. He'd also left his mobile phone behind. Without him we were stumped. In the end we had to drive away without doing a scope, which was rather unsatisfactory and put the deal in jeopardy."

Nicholls and his hard-working agent would never normally advise an owner to purchase a horse without the vital evidence a scoping can provide. Yet Foucher's stubborn resistance to his suitors sharpened Clive Smith's desire to secure a deal. He sensed that the trainer was being deliberately uncooperative because he knew the horse was exceptional and was desperate to keep him.

Smith was not for turning. After a brief consultation with Bromley and Nicholls he took a chance and decided to bid for Kauto Star without the insurance of scoping him. A price of 400,000 Euros was agreed, and while Smith was in the mood he purchased a second horse, Le Seychellois. At a stroke he had two exciting chasers for much the same price that he had offered for Garde Champetre.

Looking back on that life-changing deal Bromley has sympathy for the man who laid the foundations of Kauto Star's uplifting career. "We heard Serge Foucher was badly upset once the sale was completed and you could understand why because he knew better than anyone that the horse was a potential champion. And, of course, he was right. Maybe he was bullied a bit by the others in letting him go, but in the end he was outvoted."

Foucher confirms that he views the sale of Kauto Star with eternal regret. "Although I had a share in this horse I would never have sold him, but one of my associates wanted to sell, as did my wife. She learned that he could fetch decent money so he got sold, which made me very unhappy. They saw the money and that was it. I don't need money. Provided I can eat I am fine.

"If I am proud of one thing it is that I didn't get it wrong when I picked him out in the field from six foals. Losing Kauto Star was very painful for me because he would have been a champion at Auteuil if he stayed here. I would have won the Grand Steeplechase de Paris with him and that would have brought new horses and clients into the yard. His sale was even more painful for Jerome Guiheneuf, who rode him all the time. He took it so badly he was sick in the stomach."

Clive Smith with Kauto Star at Paul Nicholls' yard.

CHAPTER 3

HE CAME OUT A MONSTER

Kauto Star was already gambolling around a small paddock beside his dam by the time Denman was born on 17 April in the lush pastures of Corrin, Castlelyons in County Cork. To general surprise and not a little alarm to his breeders, Colman O'Flynn and his son of the same name, he was a massive foal. Both men were with the mare Polly Puttens when the foal's legs suddenly started to appear. They immediately summoned assistance from Edmond Kent, who lived barely a mile away.

"As my brother-in-law Edmond is the expert in these things, my dad was hoping he would come quickly and help pull this one out," explains the younger Colman O'Flynn. "The foal was huge all right but he had a bit of class, too."

Kent, who runs his own stud close by, adds "The call was urgent and I was at the foaling yard in three or four minutes. In my business I foal quite a lot of mares and can remember my surprise at the sheer size of the first bits I saw of this foal as we pulled away. His feet, his fetlock joints and his shin bones … they all looked enormous.

"It was tough on Polly Puttens, who was quite a small mare, maximum 15 hands 3. I knew we were going to need a bit of a pull because the mare was struggling to get the foal out. At one stage my father-in-law was looking very concerned. I'd say he thought it wasn't going to happen, and the foaling did take a bit longer than normal. Afterwards we were all panting. We were thrilled when it was over because the foal was a gorgeous creature from the start. He came out a monster and he just kept growing. He had so much bone and always had presence and scope."

Colman O'Flynn junior relates "He was a cracker of a foal and developed into a fine yearling, so big I was afraid to feed him at times. Liam Cashman, who sold the mare to us, raved about him when he saw him for the first time."

Polly Puttens had produced ten foals in as many years before she slipped a foal in October 1998. The extra long break she enjoyed may have influenced the size of her foal by Presenting. Kent suggests "Because of that she seemed to put a lot more into the next one so that he was more like two instead of one. Everything about him was extra big. He was so heavy boned he wouldn't have looked out of place at a hunt meet, but he was always athletic."

Polly Puttens was the first mare owned by Colman O'Flynn. Edmond Kent takes up the story. "My father-in-law asked me to look at two mares that were being offered from Liam's Rathbarry Stud at the Tattersalls Ireland November sale. Both were in foal. First up was a good-looking chestnut Deep Run mare, with a nice pedigree, in foal to Phardante. You had to like her.

"The second mare, Polly Puttens, aged six, wasn't so impressive to look at. She was smaller, didn't have the best pair of front legs and had run without much promise in a bumper and three hurdle races. But she was well related, and crucially was in foal to Strong Gale, a hugely successful stallion. I was a big Strong Gale fan so that clinched it for me and we bought her privately a couple of days before the sale. I think we ended up getting her for 6,000 Irish pounds."

Denman's sire, Presenting, with Frankie Dettori before winning at Kempton, April 1995.

Horses were a novelty to the O'Flynn family, who have long been dairy farmers, so there was much excitement when Polly Puttens arrived at their farmyard. Colman O'Flynn junior, explains: "I used to have a pony but she was our first broodmare. She was always cared for very well because she was our only mare when we started. She was nearly kept under the bed!"

There was a timely boost for Polly Puttens's new owners when her half-sister Natalie's Fancy won at Galway. In the years that followed Polly Puttens delivered a series of foals who progressed to be highly useful jumpers. They included Far Horizon, successful twice over hurdles, Potter's Bay and Potter's Gale, both prolific winners over fences and hurdles, and a number of other individual winners.

Polly Puttens's foal by Presenting born in 2000, later named Denman, almost broke the mould. He grew into a tall, striking, athletic liver chestnut yearling with powerful limbs though Kent recalls a minor setback in the spring of 2001. "He developed a slight bit of a bog spavin, a sprain or little swelling in his hock, so I brought him in to stand in his box for three weeks," he relates.

Once the swelling had subsided he decided to turn him out with some other young stock. It was a manoeuvre that almost cost the big yearling his life, and there is no disguising the relief in Edmond Kent's voice as he recalls: "As soon as I opened the door to the trailer he darted straight in, put his head under the metal breast bar at the front, stood up to his full height and nearly killed himself. He was so big he got under it, and when he stood up something had to give. Luckily it was the breast bar that gave way and not his back.

"Given that he was extra tall even then I still can't understand how he managed to stand up without damaging his back, maybe fatally. It was my fault and a lesson to me. I've known people lose horses like that. I still have the breast bar that he bent."

The big gelding spent the rest of the summer turned out with two yearlings who were also destined to become serious racehorses – the future Lincoln winner Babodana, bought as a foal by Kent at Newmarket, and Mattock Ranger, bred by his wife Rita, who would land the Cork Grand National in 2007. Neither would match the exploits of their companion, who was given time to mature on the family farm before he was broken in by Kent. It was an exercise which offered early evidence of an innate laziness in the horse's make-up.

He remembers: "When I was breaking him in he used to wear me out because he was so idle on the lunge and the long rein. At times it was all I could do to keep him going on the long rein. I was constantly driving him on with little effect, but when he did consent to put in some effort I could see he had a great action."

Nearly all National Hunt breeders in Ireland are sellers. Polly Puttens had already produced an impressive series of winners and now it was the turn of Denman to keep his appointment at Tattersalls Derby sale in 2004 where he was due to appear as lot 501. On paper and confirmation he looked to be one of the best on offer in the catalogue. First, though, he had to pass inspection by a panel of vets, who, to Kent's dismay, concluded that he had a wind infirmity. He wasn't totally surprised at the verdict, though he believes the decision was borderline.

Adrian Maguire, who was Denman's first trainer. He predicted that he would win the Cheltenham Gold Cup.

"When I was preparing him for the sale I was concerned that he might be a little bit coarse of his wind. It wasn't much of a problem, even on the scope, and most horses would have got away with it. Once he'd failed I asked Ned Gowing, the well-known vet, to look at him. He said the horse had a massive windpipe and would need an operation at some stage. So I took him straight from the Tatt's sale to Ned's surgery at the Curragh, where he carried out a Hobday operation, then picked him up a couple of days later and brought him home. We might have been hasty in having him operated on. I felt it was only a very minor problem but we decided to go ahead with the operation and then try him in point-to-points," he says.

After an autumn break it was time for the next stage in Denman's education. First, though, his owners had to choose a name and select a trainer. O'Flynn and several of his sons had just brought a Japanese company in Cork, called Mitsui Denman, which made batteries. Denman was the process of extracting manganese from a very hard rock imported from Chile which produces the power in batteries. Soon the four year old was registered as Denman. Adrian Maguire was at the top of their short list as trainer since his yard was barely an hour's drive away and in his time as a wonderfully brave jump jockey in England he had won on the horse's half brothers Potter's Gale and Potter's Bay.

The first approach was made by Edmond Kent in August. "I'd run into Adrian at a sale and asked him if he'd like to train Denman. He was keen to make a name for himself and I knew he'd liked the horse from a previous visit to our yard. I can remember that he almost started shaking with excitement at the prospect of training him."

Point-to-points start surprisingly early in Ireland each season. At one of the first fixtures in the Cork area, the O'Flynns made it their business to seek out Maguire to confirm the arrangement. In November, after he was broken in by Edmond Kent, Denman was taken on the short journey to Maguire's modern new stable complex in the shadow of the Baelic mountain at Laharn Cross, Lombardstown, near Mallow.

Maguire is one of the finest jump jockeys never to be champion. He arrived in England with the dramatic impact of a whirlwind at the 1991 Cheltenham Festival. On his first ride at the meeting as an 18-year-old unknown 7lb-claiming amateur he won the Kim Muir Chase on Omerta for Martin Pipe. Twenty days later horse and rider added the Irish Grand National at Fairyhouse. One of nine children of the greenkeeper at the Royal Tara Golf Club in County Meath, Maguire expected to be watching the 1991 Festival on TV at home in Ireland until a late night call-up from Pipe.

Twelve months after his astonishing introduction to English racing, by then a professional, he snatched a famous victory in the Gold Cup on Cool Ground with an aggressive, uncompromising whip-cracking finishing charge that brought immediate censure from the stewards. It seemed only a matter of time before he became champion jockey, even more so when he joined forces with the champion trainer David Nicholson.

But Maguire endured a succession of injuries that forced him onto the sidelines and prevented him achieving his ambition to be champion. In one savagely contested, no-holds-barred, stamina-sapping season in 1993–94 he rode 194 winners, but that was not quite enough to beat the title holder Richard Dunwoody, who won 197 races. At one stage that winter Maguire was 42 winners clear of Dunwoody until injury struck again. By the final day at Market Rasen the pair resembled two bare-knuckled prize fighters from the nineteenth century who had punched themselves to a standstill.

A broken neck sustained at Warwick in March 2002 brought a premature end to his career, which yielded 1,024 winners. In his quieter moments in those early days of retirement from the saddle Maguire admitted to feeling a haunting emptiness in his life. "At first I did miss the riding desperately, almost more than I can say. I thought my life was over at the time and it took me a good while to get over it. But I tipped away building the yard up and now my riding seems a lifetime ago. The buzz I got from horses like Celestial Wave winning at Leopardstown in Christmas 2006 was something else. I never thought I'd find something after riding to give me such a special feeling," he reflects.

Initially he preferred to concentrate on the oldest trade in Ireland – buying horses, bringing them along quietly, and selling them on. This involved returning to the world of point-to-points which had been his schooling ground as a youngster. He explains: "I wasn't keen to go head to head straight off with people like Willie Mullins and Edward O'Grady. I wasn't ready for that. I thought I'd let the horses take me there, if they came along."

One of the earliest arrivals at his yard was Denman in November 2004. Maguire was immediately captivated by the raw power and limitless scope of his new recruit. "The first time my eye landed on him was on the day Tom O'Mahony had taken me to meet some local breeders. Denman was only three then and I loved him at first sight," he admits.

"Anyone could have made the same judgement. You could see he was a special talent straight away. From the moment he was sent here it was obvious he had great potential, though he also had his own ideas and he came back loose from the gallops a good few times. Even so I was often ringing up Colman to say how well he was going at home."

Soon Denman's owners had the chance to see for themselves. Early in 2005 they travelled to a nearby point-to-point schooling course for a significant stage in their horse's career. When the lad due to ride Denman failed to show up the trainer took over in the saddle in a full-blown schooling session over three miles with another horse from the yard. It was a defining moment in this story.

Kent recalls: "He almost ran off with Adrian, and when he passed us after two and a half miles he was tanking. We all had smiles on our faces that day."

Maguire was bubbling as he trotted back on Denman. "I couldn't believe how strong he was at the finish," he recalls. "The further he travelled the better he felt. He could have gone round again. That's when I realised he was the real deal. We went fully three miles and although he was green he was so strong with me I was at my level best to keep him between the wings over the first five fences. Then he started to relax, and by the end I knew we could go anywhere we wanted with him. He had the lot."

After five months in training Denman was ready for his first race. Maguire booked the leading amateur, Colman Sweeney, and was full of expectation

Denman (Colman
Sweeney) wins on his
point-to-point debut
in County Cork on 20
March 2005.

Winning team... Colman O'Flynn and his family with Denman after his easy victory.

as he drove the horse to the Duhallow Foxhounds meeting at Knockardbane near Liscarroll on Sunday, 20 March. Incessant rain on a bleak spring afternoon turned the going from yielding to heavy, hardly the ideal conditions for a young recruit like Denman, but he was ready for a run. Seventeen lined up in Division Two of the five-year-old maiden but all the money was for Denman, who was backed from 2-1 to 6-4 before storming home by eight lengths from Just Naturally and two other subsequent winners.

Maguire can remember his feelings of elation as he rushed to greet his mud-spattered horse and jockey. "The way he won after leading two out I thought he had to be an absolute machine because he pulled very hard throughout and never settled at any stage of the race," he relates.

Among those watching that day was Maguire's mentor, Tom O'Mahony, a long-time friend and scout for Paul Barber, the Somerset farmer who had already won a Gold Cup in 1999 with See More Business, trained by Paul Nicholls in the picturesque yard below his house at Ditcheat where he had once milked cows. After confirming the horse was on the market O'Mahony was soon on the phone to Barber with a glowing report on Denman's potential, but initially he was put off by the asking price, which he considered too steep.

Irish point-to-points have long been a vital shop window for the country's bloodstock industry. Every meeting, however obscure, is attended by agents for wealthy English owners looking for the next big deal, the chance to make a quick buck by selling on the winner of a maiden to the major training yards across the Irish Sea. In these days of instant communications, pointers that catch the eye like Denman are invariably snapped up almost before they have been led into the lorry for the journey home from the races. Given that the horse had the physical size and scope to match his performance it remains one of the great mysteries of the turf that Denman remained on the market for six weeks without a single serious bid.

Potential buyers included Henrietta Knight and her husband Terry Biddlecombe who were at Knockardbane the day Denman won. Miss Knight famously purchased her triple Gold Cup winner Best Mate after an initial success in an Irish point-to-point and was once again searching for talented recruits. She took the trouble to inspect Denman the next day at Maguire's stables but left empty-handed, perhaps put off by the knowledge that the horse had required an operation to improve his breathing before he had raced.

Denman subsequently appeared as lot 78 in the catalogue of Brightwells Cheltenham sale on 13 April, but he was withdrawn from the auction after tweaking some muscles in his shoulder in winning his point-to-point. For Brightwells he remains the one that got away. Soon, though, Paul Barber was on his way to County Cork with Paul Nicholls, who was still licking his wounds after falling short once more in his bid to unseat the champion trainer Martin Pipe. The previous weekend Nicholls had finished runner-up to Pipe for the seventh successive year.

Barber invited Nicholls to join him on a weekend shopping trip to Ireland. On Monday 2 May they set off to watch Willyanwoody run in Barber's colours in a division of the maiden at the Muskerry Foxhounds point-to-point at Birch Hill, Grenagh in Cork. Rain poured down for much of the day and the afternoon got worse for the visitors when Willyanwoody, the 7-4 favourite, fell at the fifth fence. Salvation was at hand in the cheerful figure of Adrian Maguire who insisted the pair should take time out after racing to look at his horse that was on the market.

Nicholls recalls: "Adrian was really persistent, saying we ought to go to his place to see Denman. He wouldn't take no for an answer. He kept on and on at me until I said to Paul, 'We might as well go because we've nothing else planned.' Adrian assured us his yard was only ten minutes away by car, though we seemed to be driving for an hour and a half before we found his place."

When the visitors arrived the object of their interest was turned out in a field. He was quickly brought into the yard and briefly dressed over in his box before he was led out again for their inspection. It was still raining but no one was complaining the moment Denman walked into view.

Nicholls recalls: "The moment I saw him I was bowled over by his presence and raw power. I knew immediately I'd have him because he was just my type of horse with plenty of size, correctly put together and a lovely walker. He was just what you want if you are looking for a chaser in two years' time. Denman had only taken a few steps when I told Adrian I'd have him. The words were hardly out of my mouth before Paul countered, 'No, you won't. I'm having him.'"

Later Barber would explain; "I had to have him. Adrian told me he'd end up winning the Cheltenham Gold Cup. Of course I didn't expect that, but he was just the type of horse I like – big and strong, with some character".

A few minutes later, in the warmth of Maguire's house, the deal was done to take Denman to Ditcheat at a price of 120,000 Euros. Their host then put on the video of the horse's runaway point-to-point success. When they saw it Barber and Nicholls couldn't understand why he had not already been spirited away to England.

"The more we looked at the tape the more we liked what we saw. He pulled hard throughout, never really settled, jumped well and was running away from start to finish. In addition he was out of a mare who'd produced no end of winners," says Barber, who briefly wondered about the wisdom of buying a horse that required an operation on his wind before he ran. But that was factored into the price while Nicholls, positive as ever, pointed out that since the surgery had already been done it would save the cost of a similar operation at a later date. Once the deal was completed Barber rang a friend, Harry Findlay, who immediately agreed to take a half share in Denman.

The improbable partnership between Barber and Findlay, one a farmer, the other a gambler, is a source of endless fascination to the tabloids. They certainly make an oddball couple. One, a countryman to his fingertips, a racehorse owner for over forty years, who farms on a massive scale in Somerset and Dorset, manufactures tonnes of cheese every day and admits he is a nervous wreck if he invests £20 on one of his horses. The other is a loud, flamboyant, in-your-face extrovert who leans towards the sharp side of life, and frequently risks all on the turn of a card, a late goal, a dropped catch or a stumble at the last fence. What they share is an unconditional reverence and passion for jump racing. At first their horses ran in Barber's colours since Findlay had none of his own. Once Findlay registered silks in the name of his mother Maggie the jumpers he owned with Barber raced in alternate colours every other season.

Barber was born in the farmhouse where he now lives fifty yards above Manor Farm Stables, tucked away under a steep hill in the village of Ditcheat. As a youngster he worked extraordinarily long hours learning his trade on his father's farm. When he started in business he milked around 150 cows and

Denman as Paul Nicholls first saw him: "... I was hooked by his presence and raw power..."

The odd couple...
Paul Barber and Harry
Findlay, owners of
Denman.

produced two tonnes of milk a day. Today he milks over 2,000 cows, employs 180 people and makes 45 tonnes of cheese a day. Barber's two sons and his cousin are all central to the business, but he still remains hands on and is up long before dawn each morning checking on the various dairy herds he owns in the district, the cheese factory in the village and the workforce who make it all possible.

Racing provides his relaxation. He is equally happy at Cheltenham, Wincanton or his local point-to-point though he wouldn't cross the road to watch a flat race, is not a believer in summer jumping and cancels his *Racing Post* in the summer months. Each morning during the jumps season, however hectic his diary, he will wander down to see Denman and his other horses in Nicholls' yard.

Barber will tell you that he learned the hard way as a racehorse owner. He bought his first horse, a modestly talented point-to-point mare called Crazy Slave, for £450 and paid for her in instalments. He explains: "It was the only way I could manage because that was a lot of money to me back then." Equipped with blinkers, Crazy Slave finally won a maiden race at Badbury Rings in 1969. It was her only success.

In the early days Barber ran plenty of slow horses who failed to win, but he persevered, eventually owned an outstanding chaser named Artifice, trained by his great friend John Thorne, and dreamed of a horse in his colours taking part in the Cheltenham Gold Cup. See More Indians was the first one with the qualities to suggest he might be a Gold Cup candidate after a brilliant first season over fences. But he had to be put down in the summer of 1994 after a kick from another horse shattered his elbow while they were turned out in the cider orchard above Barber's farmhouse. Deep Bramble, bought as a replacement, did make it to the 1995 Gold Cup but he was out of his depth that day.

Fast forward to March 1998, when See More Business, owned jointly by Barber and John Keighley, paraded as second favourite for the Gold Cup. Fate then intervened when he was carried out at the third fence in an incident which was a sensation at the time. One moment he was moving with a steady rhythm towards the outside. The next his race was over after Tony McCoy felt his mount Cyborgo falter and pulled him sharply to the right to avoid the third fence, taking out his stable companion Indian Tracker and See More Business with him.

Paul Nicholls was so incensed at what happened that he confronted Cyborgo's trainer Martin Pipe a few minutes later and had to be restrained by his friend Robert Blackburn from assaulting him. Barber, in turn, was devastated at the way See More Business was abruptly removed from the race.

"That hurt me chronic, I was totally crushed", admits Barber. "I was so keyed up about the race and will never forget what happened. I hated every bit about it and I was so hurt that no one apologised to us afterwards."

At the core of Barber's dismay was the knowledge that few horses are given a second chance in a race like the Gold Cup. Yet twelve months later Barber, Keighley and Nicholls were united in triumph as See More Business, ridden by Mick Fitzgerald, galloped to glory in the same race.

Barber and Findlay met by chance at the Doncaster sales and have since owned dozens of horses together with notable success. It is an unusual alliance, as Barber readily concedes. "We live in two different worlds. He's mad as a hatter, all that punting, and no one will change him. Harry didn't know a thing about racing when we met but he's a quick learner and is totally involved now. In a way I've towed him along to some extent. He's never off the phone when he comes to see us for breakfast, sometimes betting on some cricket match on the other side of the world. He gets a bit excited all right when he's involved. I couldn't stand the strain of all that punting. Not for a minute."

Gamblers in sport don't come any bigger or more colourful than Harry Findlay. He lives on a knife edge from day to day, betting in hundreds of thousands of pounds. Once, shockingly, in 2007 he lost £2.6 million when New Zealand were bundled out of the Rugby World Cup by France in a quarter final of unbearable tension in Cardiff. How many big players could survive that kind of punishment? Findlay bets in smaller numbers these days, has won fortunes on Roger Federer and Tiger Woods and lives the kind of luxurious lifestyle most punters can only dream of achieving.

"I don't live like a king," he counters noisily. "I live better than that. I'm the luckiest bastard in the world and probably the happiest, too, because I am on a permanent high."

An atheist since the age of thirteen, he is aware that many people view the trappings of his success with distaste. "Jealousy and envy is a weakness all around us. In racing it is pandemic," he insists.

As we talked in his office, the nerve centre of his country mansion near Bath, words spilled from Findlay's lips in a torrent. When he is in full flow he is unstoppable. My companion on the big sofa in front of a bank of TV screens was a large, snoozing greyhound. Curled up in a not-so-small bundle, Big Fella Thanks looked like a pussycat, but he struck like a panther in winning the coursing Derby in Ireland for Findlay in 1999.

Naturally some bets were involved. Some hefty ones. For once Findlay was unsure of the figures as he launched into a long, heartfelt story about the dog's triumph a year to the day after the loss of two close friends in a car crash. The memory goes deep. "If Denman wins three Gold Cups it will not be a patch on what Big Fella Thanks means to me," he said.

Greyhounds have been his passion since his first visit to Slough as a 15-year-old schoolboy. "I was captivated immediately. After watching the first race I knew I was ruined. I've moved on to horses now but they will never mean as much to me as my greyhounds. Dogs become your friends for life. Horses are a buzz and a social thing."

There were many setbacks once he left school to become a gambler. He admits, "In trying to get on by gambling without a job I was almost considered a vagabond or a rogue. I was potless a million times, and homeless, too, after my mum Maggie threw me out. She and my dad were both nurses and they didn't like my lifestyle.

"Over the years I've lost my freedom, my self-respect and that of my friends and family. Yes, I've frightened myself badly. Gambling was different in those days because no one was allowed to win before the advent of betting exchanges. That's why I despise bookmakers. Look at their mentality, their greed and what they stand for. I hate them.

"Now it's possible to win if you are numerate, have the instinct and most of all the balls for it. The exchanges are transparent. Press a button on Betfair and you see how much you have won or lost and they don't close your account if you win. When I first got on Betfair it was like milking a cow. I soon built up a massive pot and thought it was the greatest game in the world, though it didn't last long."

He talks of huge coups and murderous losses in the same breath. What happens, I ask, if it all goes wrong? Could he lose everything? He takes the question on the volley. "To be honest at this stage if I had a bad losing run I wouldn't mind playing for smaller stakes. That would be a lot easier for me."

Each day he rushes headlong at bewildering speed through a diet of matches and races. At home, sitting in front of all those screens, he bets on a computer. On our journey to a local race meeting he used two phones and a network of contacts better informed than MI5. Racing is just part of it, and, surprisingly, not a particularly profitable one.

"No, I wouldn't get a living out of horses alone. I don't have much of an opinion on the form myself. I leave that to others. When you back horses at long odds-on you need to be right nearly every time," he says.

I was talking to him at Wincanton a couple of years ago during a novice chase in which he had invested tens of thousands on the odds-on favourite. As the horse moved into contention on the far bend Findlay broke off our discussion briefly and made a call to put another £6,000 on his selection. Three seconds later the horse fell. Findlay cursed and turned away.

It was a reverse to finish the bravest of punters. But soon he was bubbling again as he spoke of his two favourite sportsmen with the reverence he reserves for Big Fella Thanks. In 2000 he won £350,000 on Tiger Woods at the Open at St Andrews. He also cleaned up at 8-1 and 9-1 when Roger Federer landed the first of his Wimbledon titles in 2003.

"Tiger's victory that year paid for a house and kennels I bought near Worksop. I made a vow to have a big hit on him after he was unlucky the previous year. Yet he was so nervous as he waited to tee off on the opening

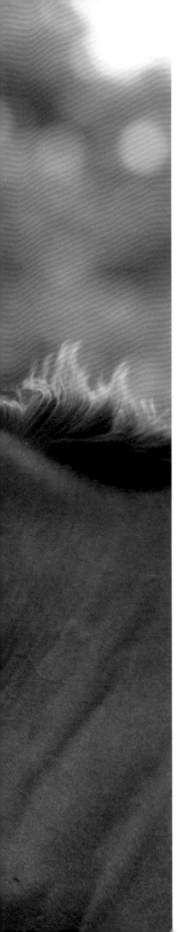

day. I know him inside out and thought, 'bloody hell. That's nice.' For the first eight holes he played like a 24 handicapper, except for his putting. In those eight holes he had a putt for par each time of eleven feet or more and banged them all in the middle of the hole with the skill of a surgeon.

"It was amazing to watch. And when he nailed a 24-footer for birdie on nine I lumped everything I had on him. I knew it was the biggest miracle of my life. For me it was £350,000 or nothing." Woods romped home by eight shots. At that stage it was the biggest ever win for Findlay.

He is also a tennis fanatic. "I rarely lose at the game because the good players are so easy to read, though Michael Stich nearly wiped me off the face of the map by beating Stefan Edburg in a Wimbledon semi-final," he admits. Part of his skill is identifying future champions. He laughs: "It wasn't hard to discover Rafael Nadal once Carlos Moya told me he was better at twelve than Carlos had been at fifteen."

His allegiance to Federer is unshakeable. He explains: "I laid out £400,000 on him to win about £300,000 in the 2005 US Open. When Andre Agassi went a break up in the third set of the final I had another lump on Roger. If he'd lost I wouldn't have been in the comfort zone to buy a horse."

Although punting is the way of life he has chosen he worries for future generations of gamblers. "Betting is going to get huge in this country. It will tempt thousands of kids leaving school. Where is the system to warn them of the dangers? It's scary and is going to be a big problem. I badly want to educate those kids at their schools, to say, "Look, if you are going to gamble, do what I tell you. Bet small and bet sensible."

In June 2010 Harry Findlay's reputation as a flagbearer for the nation's punters was dealt a severe blow when he was warned off by the BHA for six months for laying one of his horses to lose. The punishment for an offence which was widely perceived to be technical rather than deliberate immediately put an end to his owning any horses during the period of the ban.

As a shell-shocked Findlay set in motion an appeal he insisted that he would never own a racehorse in Britain again. At the hearing on July 14 his six-month disqualification was overturned and a fine of £4,500 imposed. Ahead of his appeal Findlay chose to sever his connection with Paul Nicholls, gave his share in Denman to Paul Barber in a straight swap with the Grand National fourth Big Fella Thanks, and arranged for others he owned in partnership with Barber to go to the sales. It was an unexpected conclusion to an extra-ordinary odyssey.

The look of eagles... Denman on his holidays.

CHAPTER 4

HE WAS ELECTRIC

Kauto Star stepped off the lorry at the neat little yard beside Paul Nicholls' home Highbridge early in June 2004. The trainer was surprised to discover that he was unusually tall for a four year old but also quite narrow and lean. He sensed that a long cross-channel journey after four races on testing ground inside three months might have left their mark. June is a quiet time in the Nicholls calendar. Virtually all the boxes at both yards are empty, with perhaps half a dozen still in training for summer jumping. Kauto Star would certainly not be joining them. He was bought to be a chaser, had already run ten times in fourteen months, and, felt Nicholls, would appreciate a timely summer's rest with several other youngsters in the paddock beside his house. With this horse above all there was no hurry so he remained out to grass for a further month when his companions came back into training in the second week of July.

Sonja Warburton helps Kauto Star settle into his new quarters at Paul Nicholls' yard.

Then it was a question of introducing him to the routine at Ditcheat which has delivered a conveyor belt of winners at the highest level over the past dozen years and more: first a couple of weeks walking on the roads, then one gentle canter each morning before the tempo is upped to two canters and then, finally, three times up the steep 5-furlong all-weather hill gallop stretching towards the skyline.

Sonia Warburton, in her fourth year at Ditcheat, was given the task of looking after Kauto Star. A local girl from Castle Cary, she has a quiet way with horses, which was just as well since her new charge proved to be a bundle of nerves that first challenging season.

She confirms: "He was scared of his own shadow and it took me the best part of eighteen months to overcome it. If you moved too quickly in his box he was immediately scared of you. In fact he was frightened of everything. So it was a case of doing everything slowly, carefully and calmly and gradually winning him round. It was a long time before he trusted me or anyone else."

Nicholls' early impressions of his expensive new inmate were all favourable. He was sharp in his homework, though surprisingly nervous and jumpy in his box and out with the string. At first he would dart into the corner of his box at the sight of head lad Clifford Baker and it would be many months before he settled into his new surroundings.

Kauto Star's first session in Nicholls' outdoor school at Highbridge offered an early indication of the greatness to come. French-trained horses are schooled over a variety of obstacles as a matter of routine from the age of two until it becomes second nature. So it was hardly a surprise that Kauto Star, partnered by Christian Williams, took to the school like a natural. Even so Nicholls found his pulse racing at the sight of the sure-footed horse winging ditches and barrels with nonchalant ease.

"He was electric, quite breathtaking, though he didn't waste much time in the air. If anything he was a bit too brave," he recalls.

Kauto Star was the latest smart prospect for Ruby Walsh to ride from a never-ending supply of talent unearthed by Nicholls. The partnership between trainer and jockey has enjoyed an astonishing accumulation of glory these past few years. Nicholls has frequently described their alliance as a marriage made in heaven. Yet he was turned down on several occasions by Walsh before they finally agreed a deal for the 2002-3 season.

The stumbling block until then had been Walsh's determination to continue to live in Ireland, where he is widely considered to be the finest jump jockey to emerge from that country for many years. Eventually a compromise was reached which gave Nicholls the call on his services while allowing him to continue to ride in Ireland for two or three days a week.

Ruby Walsh was born on 14 May 1979, the son of eleven times champion amateur Ted Walsh, who would go on to forge a successful career as a TV pundit while training horses from his home just across the road from the Goffs sales complex at Kill, County Kildare. To this day Ruby Walsh cherishes the memory of winning the 2000 Grand National on Papillon, trained by his father, above all others. They then shared an Irish Grand National success with Commanche Court sixteen days later. It is not widely known that the

A memorable day for father and son. Ted Walsh (trainer) and Ruby Walsh (jockey) celebrate Papillon's win in the 2000 Martell Grand National.

Walsh dynasty was almost lost to racing on this side of the Atlantic. In 1950, when Ted Walsh was four, his father, also called Ruby, decided that the family should emigrate to America, but they returned two years later and moved to their present base in 1960 where Ruby Senior trained until his death on New Year's Day 1991.

From an early age the grandson who carried his name showed signs of exceptional talent in the saddle. He was riding work before his teens but his father prevented him from taking part in point-to-points where, he believed, he would pick up more bad habits than good ones. The youngster concentrated instead on bumpers and hurdle races to such good effect that he became champion amateur in 1996–7 at the age of seventeen, and retained his title with 44 winners the following year before turning professional. Twelve months later he was champion jockey of Ireland. Ted Walsh's greatest fan would never have described him as elegant in the saddle but he was mightily effective. His son, in contrast, has been polished from the start, with the sharpest of racing brains.

Ted concedes "Comparing Ruby's style with mine in my day is like chalk and cheese. He is stylish and I was never stylish. He is a very complete rider."

Ruby's victory on Alexander Banquet for Willie Mullins in the 1998 Cheltenham Festival sealed a liaison with the trainer that continues to this day. In Ireland Walsh remains the automatic first choice of Mullins, who controls the most powerful jumping yard in the land. At the same time the jockey commutes to England up to four days a week to ride for Nicholls. It helps that he doesn't appear to suffer from pressure on the big occasion. He comments, "Some people say pressure is only for tyres but that is waffle. There is pressure but I try to use it in the right way. It is no harm to anybody and keeps you sharp."

Juggling the two roles has become an art form for Walsh. Naturally it helps that he is in constant demand though there are plenty of times when he would like to be in two places at once. He reflects: "Basically I see myself as part of two big teams. I don't take sides and try to do my best for both trainers. Nine times out of ten the big decisions make themselves. I tend to have the final say,

Ruby Walsh with his father, trainer Ted Walsh, a champion amateur jockey in his day.

but sometimes, when Paul or Willie is waiting for an answer, I might not be sure of the answer and try to avoid it."

Nicholls sensibly settles for most of Ruby Walsh rather than none of him, although the arrangement is not without its frustrations. He explains: "I think it is quite tricky for Ruby to keep us both happy. He is quite crafty and gets his sister Jennifer, his agent, to call or text me if he gets off one of mine. She is the one who delivers the bad news. Then I can't get him on the phone because he disappears!

"Normally with the top horses it works out very well and if I have one with little chance at the Cheltenham Festival I don't argue. But if I have one that I think will win I'll be very forceful that he rides it. When we do get a conflict it can cause headaches, though, as Willie says, we can't cut Ruby in two."

There was no question of Ruby Walsh missing Kauto Star's début in England. The year was drawing to a close as the horse made a profound impact in the *Western Daily Press* Novices' Chase over two miles, two and a half furlongs on 29 December at Newbury. Concerned that he made a hint of a noise as he breezed up the hill at home, Nicholls took the precaution of fitting him with a tongue strap. He was reluctant to change things because he'd always worn one in France.

The rest of the field at Newbury were the ones in need of oxygen by the end as Kauto Star jumped like a natural before darting nine lengths clear of the French-trained Foreman on the flat. Bookmakers urgently trimmed their ante-post prices about the winner for the Arkle Chase at Cheltenham in March.

Nicholls recalls, "Everyone was impressed, most of all Ruby who came back grinning from ear to ear. We both felt we had a serious Arkle candidate on our hands."

Walsh adds, "Although I'd had a little pop on him at home I didn't really know what I was getting up on. He'd arrived from France with a big reputation, but lots come with big reputations, like footballers, and don't live up to them. He bolted in that day and gave me such a feeling of exceptional power I thought he was a machine. He was only getting going from the back of the last fence. I couldn't wait to ride him in the Arkle."

For Clive Smith there was an unexpected opportunity to cash in on his investment. "I was still bubbling when Paul came up to me shortly after the race and said I could double my money on the horse. I didn't respond. Obviously he was a hot property. Half an hour later he repeated his suggestion. I don't know who he was representing and wasn't tempted to sell, not for a second. I can still remember the real buzz I got from that first win. Kauto Star showed terrific speed as he went straight past Foreman."

January tends to be the quietest of winter months for the Nicholls team, chiefly because they are all given a short break after receiving their half-yearly flu jabs at the start of the year. With meetings vulnerable to the weather the trainer eases back on the work schedule before upping the tempo again after a few weeks so that the horses peak for Cheltenham and Aintree. There was nothing dull about Kauto Star's homework that January. Everything he did on the gallops and in the schooling arena suggested he was destined for the top. Nicholls decided he needed one more race before Cheltenham. It came at Exeter on 31 January. Only two horses opposed Kauto Star, who started favourite at the prohibitive odds of 2-11, but the finish was as dramatic as anything seen at the course for years.

No stirrups. Kauto Star and Ruby Walsh were quickly reunited after falling at the second last fence at Exeter. They just failed to catch Mistral de la Cour.

All seemed to be going to plan as Kauto Star approached the second last fence, apparently still running away, but he got a shade too tight to it, clipped the top and somersaulted as he landed. Ruby Walsh was swiftly back on his feet, kept hold of the reins, ran alongside his mount, vaulted athletically into the saddle and set off in pursuit of the 20-1 shot Mistral De La Cour without attempting to put his feet in the stirrup irons.

Kauto Star and his jockey riding virtually bareback were still many lengths down as they popped over the final fence. Most jockeys would have given up the cause, but Walsh is compulsively competitive and in Kauto Star he has a partner who shares his will to win. On the flat they were catching the leader hand over fist and finished with such a flourish they flashed past the post alongside Mistral De La Cour. No one on the course was sure of the result until the photo showed that Kauto Star's astonishing late rally had failed by a short head.

Defeat in such circumstances hardly damaged his reputation, as Walsh reflected: "It is all a learning curve with novices so it is better that he learns here than in the Arkle. He's a very good horse and jumped magic all the way bar that one fence when he got in a bit deep."

There was a price to pay, however, when the horse was found to be lame behind in his box the following morning. At times like this you need a cool head and sound judgement, qualities that Nicholls' head lad Clifford Baker has in abundance. Baker worked for another champion, David Nicholson, for many years before moving to Ditcheat in 1996. He is a key player in all that happens in the yard, works prodigious hours and brings a lifetime's experience to the vital task of diagnosing and treating horses' injuries. That morning Baker suspected that Kauto Star had damaged his near hind hock, an assessment that was swiftly confirmed by X-rays which revealed a hairline fracture. The horse's season was over but there was every chance that he would make a full recovery.

The RSPCA immediately repeated its call for the practice of remounting to be banned. Their stance was supported by Best Mate's trainer Henrietta Knight, the former champion trainer David Nicholson, and perhaps, more surprisingly Clive Smith. While refraining from criticising his own jockey he questioned the wisdom of allowing riders the option to continue in a race by remounting after a fall. "If a horse falls to the ground at racing speed he is likely to be concussed at least and it is unacceptable to remount. I believe it is time for the rules on remounting to be refined," he concluded.

When Walsh jumped back on Kauto Star the horse appeared to be sound. Indeed he was still sound once he returned to Ditcheat that night. Paul Nicholls and Tony McCoy were among those who quickly leaped to Ruby's defence. McCoy spoke with the authority of a man who had remounted and finished alone on a horse called Family Business at Southwell in which all seven runners fell. The BHA eventually put an end to further discussion in 2009 by banning remounting.

Kauto Star's injury was not sufficiently serious to require surgery. Instead he was confined to box rest for the next two months to allow the damage to heal. Then early in April he was able to start gentle exercise again, at first with daily sessions on the mechanical horse walker. Once it was clear he'd made a full recovery he was turned out to grass at Highbridge early in May. Of all Nicholls' horses in the paddocks and fields at Ditcheat that summer he was the one in which his trainer invested his greatest ambitions.

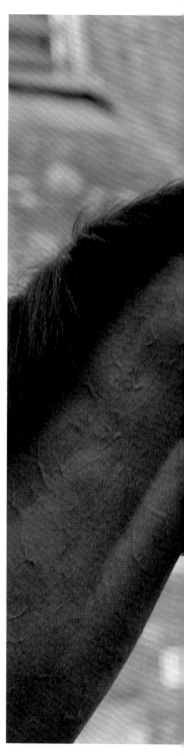

Kauto Star with Paul
Nicholls' head lad
Clifford Baker

CHAPTER 5

DENMAN MURDERED THEM

When Denman joined the Nicholls team in May 2005 there was precious little evidence of the greatness to come. He did himself so well at grass that he was as big as a bull when he was brought into training in the second week of July. He was decidedly lazy in his roadwork, lumbering along without any apparent enthusiasm or interest, and was no more impressive once he started daily canters up the hill. Nicholls soon realised he would need an enormous amount of work to bring him to full fitness.

He recalls: "He was just another horse when he started off, a bit of a fat, lazy slob if I am honest. Obviously I was learning about him but he didn't show me anything on the flat gallop or the hill, though he was a bit of a tank, could take a grip sometimes and try to run off on the bottom gallop. As he was so big and bought to go chasing we weren't even sure whether to run him over hurdles first.

"In the end we decided to give him a try over hurdles at our local track, Wincanton, to see what happened. I didn't know what to expect when he made his début in a novice race over two and three-quarter miles late in October. It was a fact-finding mission which hopefully would tell us which way to go with him."

Sunday is one of the days when Ruby Walsh prefers to ride in Ireland and Nicholls saw no reason to press his jockey to change his arrangements. Christian Williams, a tall, gifted young rider, was called up to ride Denman. He would go on to play an important role in Denman's racing education. Williams is the odd man out in a rugby-mad family. Uncle Gareth played in the back row for Wales and the British Lions. A second uncle, Owain, earned a single Welsh cap. Both were permanent fixtures for Bridgend at a time when the club was one of the strongest in the country. In addition Christian's grandad was a back row forward for Pontypridd, his father Robert was a keen player, too, until injury put an early end to his ambitions, and his brother Sean played for the under-21 Ospreys team. The links with rugby go deeper. He was in the year below Gavin Henson at school, where another pupil was the future cycling gold medallist Nicole Cook. In addition two legends of the game, Scott Gibbs and Rob Howley, live near his parents.

"Rugby is the main thing in Wales, the only thing," he reflects. "It's massive, just like racing in Eire. So everyone expected me to follow the rest of my family, yet at first I wasn't that interested in racing. I used to play centre or fly-half at schoolboy level but I wasn't quite big enough."

The boy's enthusiasm for horses was encouraged by his father, who trained point-to-pointers while running a trekking centre at his farm on the edge of Bridgend. At 16 Christian won on his début in point-to-points in 1999 on a little horse called Touch 'N' Pass who was only 15 hands 2 but a prolific winner in Wales. On leaving school he spent a winter working as a stable lad for Dai Williams, close to the Lambourn valley.

"But I was a bit wild back then and everyone said I was too big to be a jockey. I already weighed around 11 stone and at one stage it looked as though I might end up at 6' 2", so they had a point," he suggests.

Christian Williams, who rode Denman in his first two races in England.

Since a life in the saddle seemed increasingly unlikely he spent two years studying for a diploma in sports science at Bridgend College and learned plenty about nutrition, fitness and dieting which would help him combat the rigours of starvation and wasting in the years ahead. Fresh from college, still just shy of six feet, he decided to give racing a second try and started work at Richard Barber's pointing yard in Dorset. Riding winners for his new boss brought him to the attention of Paul Nicholls, who likes nothing more than to spend a spare day at point-to-points in the West Country. The next season the ambitious young Welshman moved again to join Nicholls, at first as an amateur, then as a conditional jockey.

Nicholls recalls "Christian was a typical young lad back then. He thought he knew it all and needed his wings clipping. If he'd continued the way he was he wouldn't have stayed here long but he buckled down and was often the first into the yard."

To win his long-running battle with the scales he gave up alcohol, relied on bottled water, and would go for a brisk twenty-minute walk followed by a bowl of porridge and half a grapefruit before heading off to work. In the evenings after racing he still spends an hour on a variety of exercises designed to provide core stability, improve his posture and strengthen his shoulder and back muscles.

Williams readily acknowledges the advice of Rob Howley and Scott Gibbs when they meet up at weekends in Bridgend. "Being a jockey in Wales is a bit of a novelty. I do a lot of training in particular with Rob when I am home. He was the one who gave me a programme and emphasised the importance of core strength.

"I'd say the turning point came one summer when I went home to Wales and decided to show the people who were hinting that I wouldn't make it that they were wrong. Being part of Paul Nicholls' team definitely helped. Even now he is still incredibly hungry for success and one of life's winners. I'd like to think some of that attitude has rubbed off on me," he says.

For an all-too-brief period Williams enjoyed a torrent of winners. For sheer excitement few have matched the thrill of riding Denman, a 5-6 shot, on a winning début over hurdles, though horse and rider had to work hard to see off the persistent challenge of Lyes Green by a length and three-quarters. It was hardly an earth-shattering performance but it left a lasting impression on his rider. Williams explains: "It looked as though he only scraped home but I loved him. He was green throughout, was looking to hang left on the bend after the stands towards the lorry park both times, and also drifted left with me on the final bend. It was more inexperience than naughtiness. I told Paul he was OK and would get better."

Less than three weeks later Williams's first impressions were amply confirmed as Denman trounced a highly rated hurdler, Karanja, at Wincanton in the same novice hurdle won by See More Business in 1995. Karanja, ridden by Andrew Thornton, was a short-priced favourite on the strength of some smart bumper form, and Paul Barber wasn't convinced about the wisdom of taking him on. Nicholls, positive as ever, was up for the challenge. "I can remember saying to Paul, 'Come on. Let's find out what we've got.'"

Karanja was made to look like a slowcoach as Denman pulled sixteen lengths clear of him in the closing stages. Williams followed his orders from Barber to set a decent pace in the hope of stretching his market rival, though he believed Denman would win however he was ridden. He explains: "The way I felt about Denman he'd have won even if I'd walked him out last and given Karanja a hurdle start. Everything was going to plan until the last bend when I found myself struggling to keep him straight as he hung badly left-handed. Suddenly I was concerned about getting him round the bend."

Williams swiftly pulled his whip through to his left hand and administered a sharp smack in an attempt to straighten the horse up. The response from Denman was little short of astonishing. The jockey recalls: "Before I knew it he absolutely took off with me, moved into overdrive, shot thirty lengths clear and won in a canter despite my easing him down. I had a job to pull him up."

There was a bizarre postscript when Thornton promptly lost the ride on Karanja. He recalls: "I assured the trainer, Victor Dartnall, and owner, David

Stylish debut... Denman (Christian Williams) makes a winning start in England at Wincanton, October 2005.

Staddon, that we'd been beaten by one of the best horses I'd ever seen, but I didn't get back on Karanja for almost five years."

Williams comments: "That was crazy because nothing would have beaten mine that day. When I told Paul Nicholls Denman could be the best he'd ever trained, and would win a Gold Cup, he looked at me as if I had four heads!"

Aware that the horse was still not fully fit, Nicholls felt it was time to raise his sights. The race he had in mind for Denman was the Grade 1 Challow Hurdle at Newbury two days before the end of the year until the meeting was called off at the last minute with frost in the ground. The Challow Hurdle was then added to Cheltenham's New Year's Day fixture. With a strong card already in place, the decision was taken to run it first at the unearthly hour of 11.55 yet nothing that followed in the next few hours matched the splendour of Denman's runaway victory.

This time Ruby Walsh was available for Denman, who started 5-2 favourite in the face of powerful opposition from six individual winners, most of whom had more experience than him. Carl Llewellyn set a searching pace on The Cool Guy which had taken most of them out of their comfort zone soon after halfway. Denman, however, was able to lie handy with eye-catching ease, and once Ruby Walsh began to turn the screw on him after the second last the race was as good as over. He stretched further clear with each ground -devouring stride, and by the time he reached the winning line he was 21 lengths clear of The Cool Guy, who was out on his feet.

It is impossible to argue with Harry Findlay's verdict that "Denman murdered them. That was the day we knew we had a monster on our hands. He galloped them all into the ground." Ruby Walsh was an instant convert. He has a highly entertaining turn of phrase to match his outstanding skill in the saddle and he was bubbling with enthusiasm for the horse.

"If you were told you were riding him, you'd stay in every night," he suggested. "I felt that we were only cantering all the way, yet when I looked over my shoulder on the bend I couldn't see another horse. I couldn't believe it. Although the winning distance was 21 lengths if I'd given him a flick of the whip it would have been 51 lengths. He leaped the last like the first."

Bookmakers reacted by installing Denman as the new favourite for the Royal & Sun Alliance Novices' Hurdle at the Festival at around 5-1. It was a price that continued to shorten all the way to March. The stable girl who looked after Denman that winter, and for the next two years, was Jess Allen, a strong and fearless rider, who often found her arms stretched to breaking point on him in the mornings.

"Back then it was all a bit of a game to him and he certainly had his moments," she suggests cheerfully. "He wasn't the quickest, but so big and powerful and hard to rein back when he was in full stride. He liked to try to tank away with me. And if he met a lorry on the roads he'd always want to take it on."

Nicholls' plan to bring Denman back to Cheltenham for a Grade 2 Hurdle at the end of the month was scuppered when the meeting was abandoned. As he was short of racing experience it was imperative that he have another outing before the Festival. Nicholls chose a minor race at Bangor, but any hopes of an easy passage were ended when the name of Black Jack Ketchum, unbeaten after five races, appeared among the list of runners in the morning papers. This was a match that would not have been out of place at Cheltenham. Paul Nicholls commented: "We are not going to Bangor intentionally to take on Black Jack Ketchum, but nor are we going to duck him." To general disappointment the clash didn't happen as Black Jack Ketchum was pulled out on the morning of the race. Temperatures had dropped to –6C overnight and four inspections took place before the meeting was given the green light.

In Black Jack Ketchum's absence Denman completed the formality of a lap of honour at the prohibitive odds of 1-12. The tight turns of Bangor are not ideal for a strong galloping horse with a tendency to drift wide on sharp bends, but there were no alarms this time for Christian Williams. He recalls: "I made sure I had a good lead until we had got safely round the bend after the stands. Then, once he was clear going to two out, he started hanging out to the right. Paul told me to make sure he had a good blow so I let him quicken up over the last two. Once again he gave me a tremendous feel."

Denman could only benefit from the day trip to Bangor, but afterwards Nicholls warned that he would not appear at the Festival if the going was any faster than good. Nearly all big, heavily built jump horses appreciate a decent bit of ease in the ground when they are travelling at pace. Although there are exceptions, Denman is not one of them. Pounding along on unsuitably fast ground can lead to career-ending injuries to tendons and joints. Denman's future already lay over fences, and few horses have been better equipped for the task. No wonder Nicholls wasn't prepared to take any chances along the way.

For many pundits Denman was the stand-out banker of the 2006 Cheltenham Festival in the Royal & Sun Alliance Novices' Hurdle, the opening

Overleaf: Denman (right) is beaten into second place by Nicanor at the 2006 Cheltenham Festival.

race of the card on Wednesday 13 March. If he arrived in the same form as in the Challow Hurdle, they argued, what could possibly beat him? Among those drawn to Cheltenham for this race was Denman's breeder, Colman O'Flynn, his son-in-law, Edmond Kent, and his first trainer, Adrian Maguire, who assured the *Racing Post*, "Barring accidents he'll win. In fact I'll go as far as to say he'll be one of the most impressive winners of this year's Festival. He's a special talent."

Paul Nicholls was bullish, too, as he hinted that Denman was probably the best novice hurdler he'd ever sent to Cheltenham, though he qualified that statement by adding, "What you have to remember is that he is a chaser and at one point we thought sending him hurdling would be a waste of time."

Those who invested their hard cash on Denman were in for a rude awakening as he was beaten in one of the biggest upsets of the meeting. In finishing second, two and a half lengths behind the Irish raider Nicanor, he can hardly be said to have disgraced himself. Nor was it in any way a disaster. His unbeaten record had gone, but for those prepared to look at the bigger picture he'd once again shown immense promise for the future. Yet for his trainer and his owners there was a feeling that, for whatever reason, he had not run up to his best.

Softer ground and a stronger pace would certainly have helped, yet after a mistake three from home Denman still led at the next, travelling strongly, but he was unable to resist the sustained challenge of Nicanor on the flat. The times that day suggested the ground was a fair bit faster than the official description of good, and afterwards Nicholls blamed himself for not giving Ruby Walsh more positive instructions.

He explains: "We were still both learning about the horse, and you have to remember that Ruby had ridden him in only one race up to then. I'd like to have seen Ruby make a bit more use of him down the far side. If he'd been a bit more aggressive we might have won. He wasn't convinced at the time but twelve months later he admitted that I was right.

"Maybe the horse was also over-hyped a bit because he won the Challow Hurdle so well. At the start of the season none of us thought he'd end up in that race. It was a shame Denman was beaten but I couldn't wait to start him over fences, and as he puts so much into his races we decided he'd done enough for the season."

Nicholls offers a further fascinating explanation for Denman's unexpected defeat. Liver chestnuts like him, he suggests, do not appreciate the type of bitterly cold weather experienced in the run up to the Festival. Apparently they tend to be much slower to come in their coats. That winter Denman was clipped late in January. Whatever the reason he looked unusually dull in his coat in the paddock at Cheltenham. To support his theory Nicholls checked through the form book and discovered that not a single chestnut won at Cheltenham that week.

The trainer has noticed a big difference since he decided that Denman should not be clipped any later than November. It means that he can look a bit like a giant woolly bear in the depths of the winter before his coat comes right in time for the Festival. In the weeks after his unexpected reverse at Cheltenham Denman's daily exercise was gradually reduced ahead of a long summer's break. First, though, Nicholls took the opportunity to pop him over his schooling fences. What the trainer saw fired his imagination for the challenges ahead the following winter.

CHAPTER 6

THE SPEED NUDGED 40MPH

Steeplechasers whose novice campaigns are cut short by injury can find life uncomfortably hard second time round. For the classier ones the competition can be daunting once the chance to gain vital experience against lesser lights has gone forever. The choice for their trainers is severely limited. Pitch them straight in against seasoned handicappers, often on unfavourable terms, or tackle the best at level weights in conditions races.

Even at this early stage Paul Nicholls was in no doubt that given a bit of luck Kauto Star had the qualities to go right to the top. First, though, he had to prove beyond doubt that there were no lingering legacies from the hock injury he had sustained in January.

Clifford Baker recalls, "All the signs were good because he'd never been that sore while he spent time in his box in the spring. The injury healed naturally. It was only a tiny fracture and if anything it was stronger afterwards. We had no worries on that score."

A lofty handicap mark of 149 immediately restricted options for Kauto Star's return to the racecourse. The race chosen for him on 1 November was the William Hill Haldon Gold Cup, a limited handicap over two miles, one and a half furlongs, that kick-starts the return of serious jump racing in the West Country. It promised to be a cracking renewal with a number of top-class chasers including Ground Ball, from Ireland, Ashley Brook, Monkerhostin and the triple Gold Cup winner Best Mate returning to action after an absence of ten months.

The race more than lived up to its billing as Monkerhostin pulled four lengths clear of Kauto Star on the run-in with Ashley Brook a creditable third.

Yet for so many at Exeter the day was marred by the death of Best Mate, who collapsed and died near the last fence shortly after being pulled up by his jockey, Paul Carberry.

Jump racing, by its very nature, demands so much of its heroes, both equine and human. Sometimes the price they pay is unacceptably high. Death in action for jumpers is not uncommon, but the loss of Best Mate sent shock-waves through the industry for he had been a wonderful advertisement for all that is best in the sport. Nurtured and minded by Henrietta Knight with a rare sureness of touch, he was the first to win three Gold Cups in a row since Arkle in 1964–6. Best Mate was the one who set the standard for modern-day chasers. Today a plaque guarded by flowers beside the last fence offers a poignant tribute to a great racehorse.

In jumping, as in life, the show must go on, and in the athletic shape of Kauto Star racing fans were soon to find a new hero. He was soundly beaten at Exeter, chiefly because he was in need of the outing after such a long break. That is not normally an excuse that can be offered for a Nicholls runner, but on this occasion the trainer had understandably erred on the side of caution in the horse's homework.

He confirms: "After what happened to Kauto Star in January I didn't want to be pushing too many buttons with him too early. I told everyone before the race that he was a bit short and couldn't have been happier with the way he ran when you consider that all the others were seasoned chasers while he was still a novice in all but name. He travelled really well and was bang there all the way up the straight before tiring towards the finish. I knew then he'd take the world of beating wherever we took him next."

There was already a temptation to step Kauto Star up in trip but trainer and jockey both felt that sticking to two-miles was the right option at least for the rest of the season. Positive thinking is at the core of Nicholls' unrelenting success. Aware that serious question marks surrounded the horses which had dominated the two-mile division for so long, he set his sights on the Grade 1 Tingle Creek Chase at Sandown for Kauto Star. It was a big ask but his belief in the horse was unshakeable by this point and his bold decision was influenced by his suspicion that there was a significant changing of the order in the two-mile chasing ranks. The doughty Well Chief and his own Azertyuiop were out of the picture through long-term injury while doubts lingered about the reigning two-mile champion Moscow Flyer, who would not be turning up at Sandown.

Far left: Mick Fitzgerald on Kauto Star has Tony McCoy on Ashley Brook in his sights before going on to win the William Hill Tingle Creek Chase at Sandown, December 2005

Clive Smith, Mick Fitzgerald and Paul Nicholls celebrate Kauto Star's win at Sandown.

Mick Fitzgerald with the trophy.

With Ruby Walsh sidelined by a shoulder injury Nicholls' first task was to find a suitable replacement. He considered one of his youngsters, perhaps Christian Williams, but Clive Smith, concerned at his horse's lack of racing over fences, asked him to look for a more experienced jockey. The man they chose was Mick Fitzgerald, who had won the Gold Cup on See More Business in 1999. Kauto Star caught the imagination of punters and bookmakers alike. He was immediately installed as favourite for the Tingle Creek. On the day he started joint favourite at 5-2 with Ashley Brook, with their Exeter conqueror Monkerhostin drifting out to 9-2.

Mick Fitzgerald drove down to Ditcheat four days before the race to ride Kauto Star in a schooling session. "I loved him, absolutely loved him," he said later. Concerned at the testing going at Sandown, Nicholls cautioned Fitzgerald to avoid becoming involved in a prolonged battle with Ashley Brook, a habitual front runner, partnered on this occasion by Tony McCoy. The previous evening Ruby Walsh had called with much the same advice. So much for pre-race planning.

Fitzgerald relates: "I tried to do what I was told but I soon knew I was in trouble because Ashley Brook wasn't going fast enough for us. He was flat out and Kauto Star was running away behind him, travelling like a dream. He had speed to burn. In the end I decided I couldn't disappoint my horse any longer, even though Paul was probably calling me all sorts of names in the stands."

Moving with notable ease and jumping with impressive economy of effort for one so inexperienced, Kauto Star was upsides Ashley Brook over the three Railway fences before seizing the initiative going to the Pond fence, three from home. The race was as good as over at that point, though the runner-up rallied bravely on the final hill as Kauto Star drifted left-handed under pressure. Fitzgerald reported, "We won by an easy length and a half and I told Paul the horse was a machine."

Within three days Kauto Star was the new favourite with most firms for the Queen Mother Two Mile Champion Chase at odds of around 2-1. It was a rapid promotion for the gifted young horse, who had run only four times over fences. Yet the Queen Mother seemed the logical target for him at the Cheltenham Festival, though time would show that two miles was not his optimum distance. The obvious prep race for Nicholls' new stable star was the Game Spirit Chase at Newbury early in February. When frost forced the card to be abandoned the race was transferred to Lingfield a week later.

Nicholls was anxious to give Kauto Star further experience over fences before the ultimate test at Cheltenham, but not so desperate that he was prepared to risk his horse in the glue-pot conditions which prevailed at Lingfield that bleak winter's afternoon. Soft is one thing, but Lingfield heavy is just about as deep as it can get in England. The danger in taking Kauto Star there was that he might leave his next race behind.

Instead Nicholls took him to Exeter early in March for a full-blown racecourse school, ridden by Ruby Walsh, alongside a stablemate, Cenkos, partnered by Joe Tizzard. Clive Smith travelled to Devon with his trainer. The pair then enjoyed a ringside seat of the eye-watering action from the grounds-man's truck which tracked the two horses as they scorched round the course, jumping eight fences before quickening up on the flat in the home straight. The sight of the speedo nudging 40 mph at times suggested this was a little more serious than a normal rehearsal.

For much of the journey from Ditcheat to Exeter Ruby Walsh had dozed in the back of Paul Nicholls Range Rover. But he was at his most animated

Kauto Star falls heavily at the third fence in the Queen Mother Champion Chase, Cheltenham, March 2006. Horse and rider were unscathed.

as he hosed down Kauto Star's legs in the racecourse stables after his thunderous workout.

"This horse is the real deal," he suggested, before asking, "Did you see how far he stood off the ditch? He gives you the feel of so much power underneath you. I think there is something very special about him and it will take an exceptional one to beat him at Cheltenham."

Walsh was clearly pleased to have won his own battle for fitness after spending the previous five weeks with his upper body encased in a protective jacket once X-rays revealed that he had been riding with a crushed vertebra in his back on the day he won five races at Wincanton in January. After Kauto Star's memorable workout at Exeter on 1 March nothing would prevent his jockey taking his place in the saddle at Cheltenham two weeks later.

Many visitors to Ditcheat that spring pressed the trainer for his views on Kauto Star and Denman. His confidence in both was rock solid, but he was in for a rude awakening. Both attracted huge volumes of support in the ring on Wednesday 15 March and in the space of seventy-five minutes both were undone. No wonder old timers will tell you that training racehorses involves months of misery and moments of magic. Compulsively competitive by nature, Nicholls is far too positive to accept that gloomy view of his occupation. Normally he is the one who provides the magic, but when the results go against him the wounds run deep.

His black mood after the defeat of Denman in the opening race was briefly lifted by the stylish success of another fine prospect, Star De Mohaison, in the following race, the Royal & Sun Alliance Chase. One moment his spirits were on the floor, the next they were soaring again as Star De Mohaison returned in triumph.

His euphoria didn't last long, for Kauto Star was out of the Queen Mother Champion Chase almost before it had begun. The third fence in this race is directly in front of the stands. Travelling keenly just behind the leaders, Kauto Star stood off too far, dived at the fence, burst grotesquely through the birch and plunged headlong to the ground in a horrifying fall which brought down Dempsey. Errant hooves then struck him as the remaining runners thundered past. It was the kind of fall that can kill, and there was general relief all round when Kauto Star and Dempsey galloped away apparently unscathed and their jockeys rose shakily to their feet.

"He took it by the roots," reported Walsh as he wandered disconsolately back to the weighing room. Newmill was a worthy winner that day, but much of the post-race focus centred on Kauto Star and his dramatic early exit.

Nicholls told reporters, "He's fine and lives to fight another day. Maybe his slight inexperience at this level caught him out. At six he has plenty more chances ahead of him. I suspect it was a case of being a bit too racy, too bold and brave, which is a trait that has followed him through his career. He's still short of experience and tends to step at his fences a bit."

The trainer mentioned the possibility of taking Kauto Star to Aintree, but that was not an option once the horse arrived home that night as his off-hind fetlock joint came up like a balloon and there were other lumps and bumps in evidence. Nicholls recalls, "He looked a bit of a sorry sight, with signs of others having galloped all over him on his hind leg. It was much like someone stamping on your ankle. Extremely painful."

For Sonia Warburton the sight of Kauto Star being trampled was deeply distressing. She admits, "It was bad enough at the time, and when I watched it again on the video it was horrible. I realised how lucky he'd been to survive. Afterwards he was feeling very sorry for himself. He was battered and bruised, with hoof marks all over him."

Initially Nicholls and Clifford Baker feared the horse might have broken something in his fetlock, but a series of X-rays were all clear. Baker then spent much time hosing down the joint with cold water to ease the bruising. Once that started to disperse, Kauto Star was soon on the move again, first on the horse walker, then at light exercise. For him another season had ended prematurely but he recovered so well from his injuries that he was schooled over fences before being turned out in the paddock at Highbridge.

That summer Nicholls spent much time mulling over future options for Kauto Star. Uncomfortably aware that he had yet to find the key to the horse, he suspected that he would benefit from a step up in trip. At times, he concluded, he'd been too impatient for his own good. That had certainly played a part in his downfall at Cheltenham. As a four year old, he'd beaten the best of his age over two and a half miles in deep ground at Auteuil. Now, more than two years later, he was surely ready for longer distances again.

CHAPTER 7

DENMANIA

In the early days at Ditcheat dry autumn weather often restricted Nicholls' opportunities to give his horses practice over fences ahead of their races. Matters improved the moment he built his own outdoor schooling arena beside his home at Highbridge. The surface, which is harrowed every day by assistant trainer Dan Skelton, is so forgiving you could send a fleet of horses over the two jumps every day of the year without a moment's worry.

Here raw youngsters, bumper winners and horses from the flat are taught to jump until they can do it as a matter of routine. Watching them bound round the school is a delight. One moment they are soaring over a fence,

Ruby Walsh puts Denman through his paces in the schooling arena at Ditcheat in 2006.

four strides later they are into a tight turn which takes them to another obstacle on the far side. They start over small brush fences and soon graduate to ditches which are often filled with bright blue plastic barrels to help them concentrate. They will go left-handed for a couple of minutes, then right-handed.

Usually they are ridden by Nicholls' ever-expanding band of regular jockeys, men like Christian Williams, Daryl Jacob, Nick Scholfield and Harry Skelton. If they are away racing or injured then conditionals like Ian Popham or amateurs like Ryan Mahon get their chance. Occasionally, if you are really lucky, you will watch a master-class in schooling conducted by Ruby Walsh. The horses he rides go at his pace, not theirs, with his hands dropped neatly onto their necks so that he does not seem to interfere with their mouths at any stage. Free-wheeling novices, hardy old handicappers and Gold Cup winners all seem to jump well for Ruby Walsh, who loves what he does with a passion, does it wonderfully well and has brought great joy to others in the doing of it.

It was here, in this school in the autumn of 2006, that Denman again set the pulse of his trainer racing as he winged over every type of obstacle that he faced. For a big, tall, long-striding horse the school is, in all honesty, tight enough; but from the start he jumped everything put in front of him like a natural and bounded round the sharp bends like a high-class athlete.

Sam Thomas gets to know Denman at Ditcheat in 2006.

At the start of the campaign Denman was moved to the box next to the one occupied by Kauto Star in a part of the yard beside the main entrance known as Millionaire's Corner. The switch was a tacit acknowledgement by Clifford Baker and Paul Nicholls of his elevation to the stable's elite squad of horses.

The logical target for Denman that second season was the Royal & Sun Alliance Chase over three miles at Cheltenham in March. It had already been in the diary for months. In the circumstances it was quite a brave decision by Nicholls to begin Denman's fencing career over little more than the minimum distance of two miles at Exeter at the end of October where he would be taking on the speedy Penzance, winner of the 2005 Triumph Hurdle.

Nicholls explains: "Yes, it was some way short of his best trip but sometimes you can start off stayers over a bit shorter on a stiff track. Denman has always been a hard horse to get fit, so making his début over a shorter distance was going in our favour a bit, and from what I'd seen at home his jumping was the least of our worries."

Ruby Walsh and Paul Nicholls were in unstoppable form at Exeter by the time they met in the paddock with Paul Barber and Harry Findlay before the William Hill Casino.com Novices' Chase. Jockey and trainer had already shared a double that afternoon with Beau Michel and Ornais. Nicholls does not normally need to give Walsh orders as both men invariably think as one on tactics involving their horses. The priority on a first run over fences, as always, was a clear round.

Keen and on his toes, Denman, the 3-1 on favourite, played up at the start, causing a moment's anxiety before consenting to set off. He was in front as early as the third fence and won easing up by ten lengths from Penzance. It was a thoroughly workmanlike introduction for a horse whose pedigree is laced with stamina. Walsh would have preferred a lead for much longer but with Denman pulling so hard and nothing willing or perhaps able to take the field along he sensibly allowed him to stride on. He was briefly headed four out by Penzance where he was less than fluent and was clumsy again at the next fence but he was back in front by then and soon fully in command though there was a hint of an old habit as he drifted left approaching the final fence.

Later Nicholls concluded, "He didn't win doing triple handstands or anything like that and there seemed to be one or two doubters afterwards, but I couldn't be happier with him as I'd left plenty to work on. We always knew he'd be plenty free enough, and he was also just a bit green in front. I've always though he'd be better left-handed, too."

Bookmakers were sufficiently impressed to install the winner as 5-1 favourite for the Sun Alliance Chase. Nicholls hoped the race would put an edge on Denman, but to his surprise, and no little concern, instead of shedding unwanted pounds like a dedicated slimmer with one eye on the scales, the horse actually put on a little weight before his next appointment at Cheltenham over two and a half miles.

This time he faced a much sterner test against the smart Don't Push It, ridden by A.P. McCoy, with several other promising types in the line-up. Denman's jumping wasn't entirely foot perfect but he again travelled strongly

and despite veering markedly left-handed he was not for passing as Don't Push It laid down a serious challenge on the flat.

Ruby Walsh reported, "He was just bowling along enjoying himself and doing nothing in front. But when you want him he does pick up."

Paul Barber then asked his jockey the question uppermost in his mind. "But does he stay, Ruby? Will he stay three miles?"

Quick as a flash Walsh replied. "This horse will stay six miles."

Nicholls suggested, "He has probably learned more today than in any race he's had because he really had to knuckle down to the task before staying on strongly up the hill. Don't forget he's still amazingly green, so races like this are the only way he is going to learn. I don't see the need to step him up to three miles just yet."

That winter Denman took to tanking along the bottom gallop at Ditcheat so powerfully that his trainer or his assistant Dan Skelton would stand at the end of the chute waving their arms energetically to ensure that he started to ease down before coming to any harm. Jess Allen, the strongest of riders, explains:

Ruby Walsh, Paul Barber and Paul Nicholls salute Denman's victory in the Sun Alliance Chase at Cheltenham 2007.

"Whenever he did a piece of work there he was so competitive he wouldn't pull up until he'd gone ten lengths clear of his galloping companion. The first time it happened he scared me and even when I got used to it I didn't feel in control."

The evidence of Cheltenham persuaded Nicholls that Denman needed more racing experience, sooner rather than later. A novice chase at Newbury on 26 November proved to be his third inside a month. This time he had a new jockey. A day earlier Nicholls and Walsh shared a treble at Newbury, but on that Sunday Walsh was riding in Ireland for Willie Mullins. This gave a chance to Sam Thomas, the stable's new number two jockey, who drove to Ditcheat to get to know Denman in a schooling session.

Thomas had become an important addition to the Nicholls team as a replacement for Christian Williams, who injured his shoulder so seriously in a horrifying fall at Worcester in September 2006 that his career hung in the balance for many months. The previous season he had ended high in the jockeys' table with 79 winners. Now his future was on hold after a horse called The Spacer fired him into the ground with sickening force twenty-four hours before he was due to start riding out again at Ditcheat.

Williams recalls, "I hardly remember anything about it, which is probably just as well as I'm told the horse lay on me for a while. I knew I was in big trouble."

Three bouts of surgery followed in a month, the third one lasting nine hours as nerves from his leg were used to replace those that had snapped in his shoulder. Afterwards he was so seriously ill he remained in a higher intensive ward for ten days. As his long road to recovery began from his X certificate fall there was a vital question that Williams dared not voice. It is one that every jockey faces when he is at the crossroads. Would he be allowed by doctors to ride in a race again? And would he be every bit as effective after intricate surgery to repair his shattered shoulder?

Aware that no one would know the answers to these questions for many months, Nicholls signed up Thomas as back-up for Ruby Walsh. Bright and articulate, Sam Thomas comes from a family of teachers in a remote village between Hereford and Abergavenny. His parents, Geoff and Dot, are both retired head teachers and his two sisters also teach, but his heart was always set on racing.

"As a small boy I was quite independent," he recalls. "If I had something I wanted to do I'd end up doing it. My dad took me racing all the time and it really stuck. By the time I was ten I was so dedicated about being a jockey I'd only eat salads at home for weeks on end to stay light. And when my dad said I'd never make a jockey because I couldn't get out of bed in the mornings, I was up at five the next day galloping my pony round the field in the pitch dark."

Thomas progressed though pony club and hunting to point-to-pointing, though he remains to be convinced that this particular route is the best way forward for a budding jockey. "It is difficult to make any impact in points if you don't have the right contacts," he explains. "My dad bought me a point-to-pointer, which was a big help, but I was also riding some real rubbish at one stage and that can do a lot more harm than good. You get to learn bad habits on bad horses and it is hardly fun riding the ones that can't jump.

"There is no easy way to make your name because stables tend to have their own jockeys. So when you start out you have to take what is offered. I think youngsters beginning in point-to-points now should try to pick and choose, and try not to ride anything unless it has a chance. Otherwise they might end up losing their bottle before they start."

Out clear... Denman and Ruby Walsh at Exeter in October 2006.

Thomas left school at 16 with nine GCSEs to become a stable lad. He progressed to become an amateur jockey riding for Venetia Williams, turned professional in 2003 and was already established as a rider with a future when Nicholls came calling. He didn't take long to accept. "The way I saw it, being a No. 2 with Paul Nicholls was really like being a No. 1 elsewhere, and I hoped my day would come," he concluded.

Thomas began riding out at Ditcheat, schooling regularly on his visits, and soon found himself on a regular supply of classy jumpers on the track. There wasn't a young jockey in the country who wouldn't have changed places with him. He was already enjoying a lucrative campaign with Nicholls when he was told he'd be riding Denman at Newbury.

Only three took him on in the Berkshire Novices' Chase over two and a half miles on heavy ground, the most testing he had encountered so far. Odds of 2-11 suggested the race was little more than a formality for the big horse and his new jockey, but Thomas would have been less than human if he didn't experience a frisson of nerves on the way to the start. It helped that Snakebite made the running to half-way before Denman jumped into the lead at the ninth fence. After that it was more a case of schooling in public as he cruised home with any amount in hand. It was enough to persuade Nicholls to give him a Christmas break before bringing him back into full training in time for Cheltenham.

All season Harry Findlay had been setting himself up for a major touch on Denman at the Cheltenham Festival. Getting his bets on with bookmakers was the hardest part. He put in friends to snap up the best ante-post prices available and topped it up whenever he found a bookie prepared to take him on. As the horse's odds shortened through the winter months his trainer concentrated on bringing him to his peak for the third week in March. If he felt any pressure from Findlay's extraordinary betting activities he wasn't admitting it.

He says, "Obviously I was aware of Harry's punt because he doesn't exactly keep these things quiet. He's enthusiastic in everything he does but I don't feel under pressure if I know he has had a fortune on one of mine because he knows I am doing my best anyway."

Denman's relentless rise towards the top of the chasing tree was not without controversy. For his warm-up race before Cheltenham Nicholls chose a three-mile race at Newbury on Totesport Trophy day. Nicholls knows the programme book from back to front for the good reason that he still insists on making all the entries for the horses. Aware that the Toteplacepot Novices'

Chase was normally a Class 2 event for those who have not won more than two steeplechases, he was delighted to spot in the racing calendar that the conditions had changed to allow any novice to run. For Denman it was an ideal opportunity shortly before the Festival.

Others were not happy at the change in conditions. They included Charlie Egerton, an eccentric old Etonian who had pinpointed this very race for his own promising candidate Mr Pointment. The horse's owner, Anton Johnson, a hairdresser from Warrington, wasn't slow to voice his irritation to the *Racing Post*.

He said, "It looks to me as though because Paul Nicholls is bringing all his best horses, including Kauto Star, to Newbury they have done this to accommodate him. I can see the benefits of having Denman there because he is a crowd puller, but what is the point of having a programme book in the first place? We will run anyway, but now we've got to take on a horse of Denman's class it leaves a sour taste," concluded Johnson who, ironically, within months would transfer Mr Pointment from Egerton to Nicholls.

Ruby Walsh flew over the day before Newbury to school a number of horses, including Kauto Star and Denman. In his highly informative weekly column in the *Racing Post* Nicholls hinted that Denman would improve enormously from the run after a ten-week absence even though he had worked him hard. With so much at stake he was relieved the meeting was on despite forty-eight hours of snow and rain.

Denman was the first to strut his stuff with a spectacular display that saw his odds shorten again for Cheltenham. He was soon bowling along in front of his two rivals, flicking over the big Newbury fences without disturbing his rhythm. Long before the end he was out on his own and cantered home hard on the bridle thirty-six lengths ahead of Mr Pointment, a solid yardstick, with the startling distance of ninety-three lengths back to the third Standin Obligation, winner of nine of his twelve races. As horse races go it came embarrassingly close to a walkover.

The result was a welcome boost to Harry Findlay, recently returned from his annual winter break in Australia which always takes in the Australian Tennis Open. He steamed into Denman at all odds down to 3-1 on, and never had a moment's anxiety. "That was just like buying money and helps make up for all the dosh I've lost on Australia in the two recent one-day cricket internationals," he concluded.

The first day of the Festival proved a frustrating one for Nicholls. Several horses ran well, but not quite well enough, and his afternoon was encapsulated by the fall of Twist Magic, who came down two from home in the Arkle when holding every chance. The following day Nicholls saddled Silverburn and his year older full-brother Denman in the opening two races. Silverburn, already winner of the Tolworth Hurdle, didn't let the family down by finishing a creditable fourth in the Ballymore Properties Hurdle.

Then it was the turn of Denman, whose coat, this time, was gleaming with condition as he was led round the paddock by Jess Allen. In the ring the big hitters, perhaps encouraged by the bullish comments of Harry Findlay, piled into him at 11-8 and 5-4 and finally 6-5 as if there was no settling day. Findlay had taken a large hospitality box in the temporary enclosures close to the last fence and was entertaining dozens of punting friends. For several weeks he'd been telling anyone who would listen that Denman was an absolute certainty.

A class apart. Denman and Sam Thomas cruise to victory at Newbury, November 2006.

"He's a monster bet," he suggested to every journalist that sought him out. In this mood Findlay is unplayable. He speaks without fear of contradiction or interruption. "I've been smashing into him for months at all odds down from 10-1 and with the opposition so weak will keep doing so until he goes odds on," he added.

So often in sport the performance does not live up to the hype. Not this time. Denman was every bit as dominant as his legion of supporters dared hope as he dismantled his rivals one by one with a ruthless exhibition of jumping at pace. He was in the firing line throughout, though the unconsidered outsider Eurochancer briefly blazed the trail over the first three fences. The favourite then took over, pounding along at such a powerful tempo the field behind him were soon stretched out as far as the eye could see.

Aces Four, ridden by Graham Lee, was the only one equal to the challenge on the drying ground that clearly suited him so well. He showed in front for the first time at the eleventh fence and did his best to force the pace for the next mile. But the menacing figure of Denman was always at his shoulder, and when the leader stumbled on landing at the third last fence the race was all but over. Denman galloped on relentlessly, winged the remaining two fences, and stormed up the hill as if he could have gone round again.

The quality that sets Denman apart is his ability to maintain a lung-bursting gallop to the point where others are no longer able to follow. And when Aces High all but came down three out he was left to come home in splendid isolation. Ferdie Murphy, trainer of the runner-up, claimed that his horse had still not been asked a question when he came down but, in truth, the best he could have hoped for was second prize.

In a world of their own...
Ruby Walsh and Denman
jump the fourth last well
clear on their way to a
runaway victory at Newbury,
February 2007.

As the winner came back to a riotous reception we witnessed the first recorded outbreak of Denmania. In a moment of lucidity amid all the chaos Findlay admitted to having won just under £1 million.

"The ante-post gamble was all down to Alan King," he suggested mysteriously before providing an explanation. "After the Festival last year I felt there were only two horses who could win this, and suddenly King decides that My Way de Solzen is not running as he's been switched to the Arkle instead. That was the cue for us to take the 10s, the 7s and 6s, all the prices down. Thanks to Alan King we've landed a massive touch. He must be happy, too, after My Way landed the Arkle on the opening day," he said.

The ever-increasing demands of the modern media machine allow owners and trainers precious little time to enjoy the moment on these occasions. Nicholls had scarcely finished shouting Denman home before he was besieged by camera crews and reporters seeking his views. Above all they wanted to discover when chasing's new star would meet Kauto Star, who was set to tackle the Gold Cup forty-eight hours later. Nicholls, sensible fellow, had known the answer for months but he had no intention of sharing it with the rest of us just yet.

He explains, "With Kauto Star still to run it wasn't the time for me to be talking about plans for the two horses. I was just happy to be celebrating a brilliant win by Denman, who was still a big baby."

In their haste to drum up business, bookmakers were already issuing their ante-post odds for the 2008 Gold Cup before the 2007 race had taken place. Betfred's odds of 9-1 about Denman disappeared quicker than it takes to tell, and soon 6-1 was the best available. As the connections of the winner stepped up to the podium to collect their trophies three cheers rang out for the horse who had delivered the dream for them. That brought an emotional response from Paul Barber, who called out "This is for the Odd Couple."

Walsh was full of praise for Denman. "He's improved so much and he's a great jumper. He never lost an inch going down the back but he's not straightforward. He's a character, a quirky, leery horse."

There was never much chance of Denman running again after Cheltenham, though he held an entry for another important prize at Aintree a month later. Aware that he is a horse who puts his heart and soul into every race Nicholls was more than happy to rest him until the following season. In his absence Aces Four advertised his form in the strongest possible fashion by running away with the Mildmay Novices' Chase.

Nicholls reflects: "He's such a big horse you have to put a lot into getting him fit; you have to do a lot of miles with him at home, just like athletes at the Olympics who do no end of training over many months to bring them to peak fitness on the day that matters. Denman is not a horse who has an easy race. He'd had five hard races. That was enough."

The moment that ignited the first outbreak of Denmania. Ruby Walsh and Denman win the Sun Alliance Chase, March 2007.

CHAPTER 8

A £1 MILLION BONUS

In the early stages of their careers Kauto Star was always one step ahead of Denman. French-bred jumpers, used to schooling on almost a daily basis by the time they are two or three, are invariably more precocious than store horses reared on thousands of farms and studs in Ireland where time is never so important.

Kauto Star had not reached his third birthday when he raced for the first time in March 2003, and he'd already run in ten races in France before Denman was broken in by Edmond Kent. In terms of experience the gap between them at that stage was more like a yawning chasm, but in the years that followed Denman, a typically late-maturing Irish National Hunt type, would eventually start to make up for lost time. In October 2006, when Kauto Star was preparing to begin his third season as a chaser, Denman had yet to jump a fence in public. Both would make relentless progress that season.

The race Paul Nicholls chose for Kauto Star's return to action was the Old Roan Chase, a limited handicap over two and a half miles at Aintree, a flat track with tight turns that tends to play to the strength of speed horses. Pace, not stamina, is what is required. Although Nicholls was still open-minded about Kauto Star's best trip at this stage he had no concerns about stepping him up in distance. Aware of his jumping frailties in the past, he put him through a course of intensive schooling in his arena at Highbridge. The message from Nicholls ahead of Aintree was typically upbeat. "He's schooled beautifully, has shown no ill effects from his fall at Cheltenham and I think he will relish the trip," he said.

Kauto Star justified his trainer's faith with a stellar performance that immediately pitch-forked him close to the summit of the chasing tree. Giving weight all round, he glided through the race with eye-catching ease,

coasted into the lead after three from home and, despite diving awkwardly through the last fence, won hard held by Ruby Walsh by twenty-one lengths from his stable companion Armaturk. Crucially the winner was chock-full of running at the finish. Hard-nosed form book students, who deal solely in pounds and lengths, might have questioned the value of the form, but it was the style and ease of Kauto Star's success that demanded your attention that day.

The bookies took notice as they promoted Kauto Star to the head of the market at 7-2 for the King George V1 Chase on Boxing Day. At the same time he remained 5-2 for the Queen Mother Champion Chase and was shortened to 10-1 for the Gold Cup. Watching on television from his local track at Wincanton, Paul Nicholls admitted that he was tempted by the prospect of taking Kauto Star to Kempton. "Winning like that opened up all sorts of options for him. Ruby and I both felt he was a King George horse. My first

Kauto Star with Ruby Walsh on their way to a thunderous success at Aintree, October 2006.

Overleaf: Sonja Warburton parades Kauto Star after his commanding victory in the Betfair Chase at Haydock, November 2006.

NORTH WEST MASTERS

HAYDOCK PARK AINTREE

betfair million

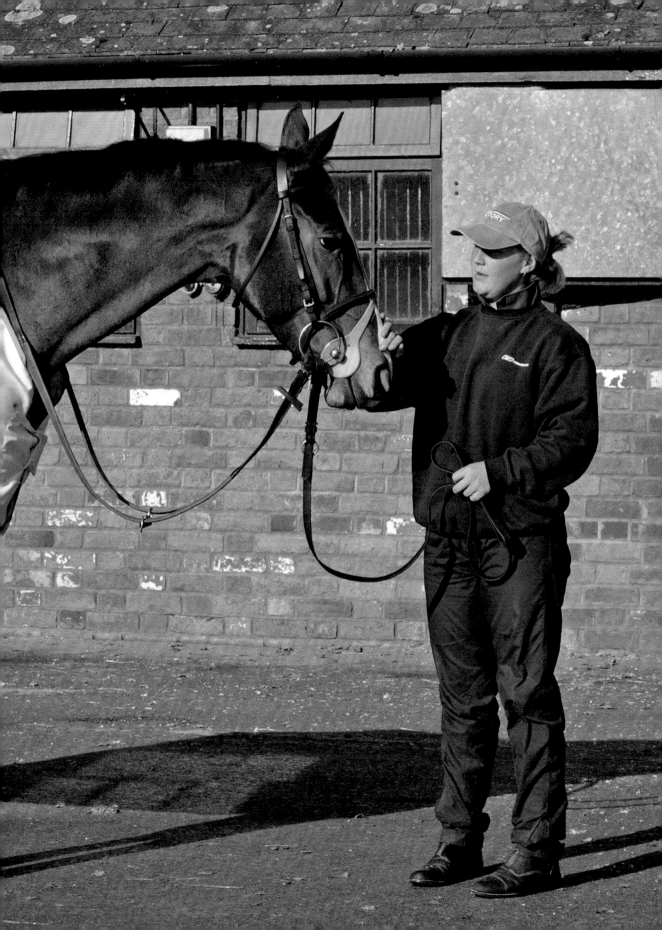

thoughts were that he could take in the Tingle Creek Chase first at Sandown on 3 December," he said.

Within days the trainer had all but ruled out another tilt at the Champion Chase in March. The horse himself was in such rampant form at Ditcheat that soon Nicholls decided to raise his sights and pitch him against some of the best staying chasers in training in the Betfair Chase at Haydock on 18 November. Kauto Star would be moving into unknown territory by attempting three miles for the first time, but Nicholls felt he was ready for the challenge as you could readily pick holes in the form of most of the leading contenders, most notably L'Ami, from France, and Beef or Salmon, from Ireland, who both tended to come up short on their visits to England.

Besides there was the not inconsiderable lure of a million-pound bonus provided by Betfair for the horse who landed this race, the King George and the Gold Cup. The Betfair Million was not the reason that Kauto Star was switched to Haydock, but it would be unrealistic to suggest it was not at the back of Nicholls' mind when he made the entry.

He recalls: "As we were heading for the King George the next step was to try him at three miles, so Haydock, which is not a stiff track, was the obvious place to go. If the ground didn't come up testing, the Betfair Chase was ideal to show us if he stayed three miles. My gut feeling was that he would stay. Ruby Walsh felt so too, but there was only one way to find out and Clive Smith was all for having a go. The £1 million bonus was a terrific initiative, and if he won well we'd have to start thinking about it as he was already favourite for the King George."

The 2006 Betfair Chase proved to be the defining moment of Kauto Star's uplifting career. His start was efficient, his jumping outstanding and long before the end he was running in a race of his own. At the line he was seventeen lengths clear of Beef or Salmon, winner of nine Grade 1s. He looked in such a different league to the others that Betfair's accountants must already have been resigned to sending a massive cheque to Clive Smith in March.

Bookmakers clearly believed that Kauto Star could do it. They offered only 5-4 against him winning the King George and 3-1 that he scooped the massive pot offered by Betfair by adding the Gold Cup. Nicholls certainly seemed to have stars in his eyes as he discussed the prospect of landing the jackpot with Kauto Star.

"We'll give it a go now that he has proved that he stays every step of the three miles. I thought he was awesome. It was an amazing display, totally breathtaking. Deep down I thought he could win it but I was a bit shocked at how he was in total command from some way out. I didn't need to ask what Ruby thought. A glance at his face as he came back in smiling broadly was enough to tell me he already felt the Gold Cup was ours for the taking," he said.

Walsh has seldom been so animated in triumph. He looked like a man who was holding a winning ticket on the lottery, which, in a sense, he was. "Kauto Star was lobbing but when I switched him on going to the last fence he felt like a horse who had just jumped in at the start. He can go all the way," he predicted.

Clive Smith will never forget the look on the face of Paul Nicholls that day as they rushed to greet Kauto Star. Paul kept saying, "We might have a world-beater here," he recalls. Smith had already backed his horse for the Gold Cup at the indecently long odds of 140-1 on Betfair and would continue to support him as his price shortened in the months that followed.

For Smith, Nicholls and Walsh all roads seemed to lead to Kempton on Boxing Day. That was the plan agreed with Clive Smith before he jetted off for a brief holiday. Within days he had a startling change of heart. Initially he sent a text to his trainer suggesting that Kauto Star should be allowed to try to win the Tingle Creek Chase for a second time.

It is fair to say that at first the idea didn't appeal one bit to Nicholls. He texted Smith, explaining that there was only a fortnight between Haydock and Sandown. More to the point, he questioned the wisdom of bringing Kauto Star back to two miles after seeing the benefits of running him at longer distances. The horse had finally learned to settle in his races. Why risk revving him up again and jeopardise his chance of scooping the Betfair Million?

Smith, however, would not be denied. One of those enthusiastic owners who enjoys having an input in the plans for his horses, he believed that the Tingle Creek was Kauto Star's for the taking and pressed Nicholls to think again. Still far from certain about such a dramatic change of course, the trainer sought the opinion of Ruby Walsh, who at first agreed with him. "It's not a great idea because it will only get him racing too keen in the King George. Don't do it," advised the jockey.

Within minutes Walsh had changed his mind. He rang Nicholls back, urging him to run Kauto Star at Sandown. "We've got to go. We might all be dead next year," he suggested by way of explaining his rapid U turn. As the debate continued over the next forty-eight hours Smith was gradually winning the argument. The horse was already entered, the race at Haydock appeared to have taken nothing out of him, and he would be a raging hot favourite on testing ground that should help to take the sting out of the two-mile specialists. By Friday Clive Smith's diplomacy had gained the day. Barring a last-minute drama his horse would run.

Moments after Kauto Star strengthened his reputation by pulverising the opposition in the Tingle Creek, his trainer paid tribute to the persistence of his owner. "Full marks to Clive. At first I was against bringing the horse here after he'd shown he stayed so well last time, but he wouldn't take no for an answer and he's been proved right. When I looked at the race this morning I'd have been irritated if his name was missing from the runners. We were entitled to bring him here because he was bouncing at home and had a favourite's chance. You don't have horses to leave them in their boxes. We race them, but there was no gamble in running him because if I'd had the slightest doubt he would have stayed at home."

The victory was not entirely without blemish. Kauto Star survived two mistakes, most notably a careless error at the second last that would have brought lesser horses to a halt. Yet, if you blinked, you missed it. He recovered immediately and cruised clear of Voy Por Ustedes who had won the Arkle Chase in March and would go on to land the Queen Mother Champion Chase in the spring. The form was gilt-edged. All distances seemed to come alike to the flamboyant chaser who was now ante-post favourite for just about every major event in the months ahead except the Boat Race.

It was still too premature to mention his name in the same breath as Desert Orchid, but those closest to Kauto Star did not doubt his potential to dominate the sport. Eyes shining with delight, Walsh declared "He's an exceptional horse who jumps brilliantly and has loads of gears. Long before my time they talked in glowing terms of Arkle working alongside his stable companion Flyingbolt. That is the level of this fellow. Although he belted the second last he never looked like lying down. He's learned from past mistakes."

Nearby Nicholls was conducting an impromptu press conference secure in the knowledge that he was the one holding all the aces. "We have several options at Cheltenham with Kauto Star and we don't have to go for the Gold Cup," he suggested. "If it was bottomless we could look at the Champion Chase or the Ryanair Chase."

First, though, an enticing appointment beckoned at Kempton on Boxing Day where cars are invariably still queuing to enter the course as the runners

circle at the start for the third race. Strictly on form it was hard to see beyond Kauto Star, who was rock solid in the King George market at 8-13. With not a single past winner of the race in the line-up for the first time in twenty years it was difficult to nominate serious dangers to the favourite. On official ratings there was none to touch him.

Champion jockey Tony McCoy, on the 9-1 shot Exotic Dancer, pinpointed one area that might offer him hope though you sensed he was clutching at straws as he suggested, "The one plus we have is in the jumping department. Kauto Star can make mistakes, so that is a possible opening for us, but he will be very hard to beat."

There was no sign of jumping frailties when Ruby Walsh schooled Kauto Star over twenty fences on the Thursday before Christmas, an open ditch ten times and a plain fence ten times. Nicholls will tell you that the horse has never put a foot wrong in the outdoor school. The jumping errors, when they came, were at the racecourse.

Nerve tingling... Kauto Star and Ruby Walsh survive a serious error before going on to win the Tingle Creek Chase at Sandown for the second time, December 2006.

Sure enough Kauto Star delivered two of the most alarming gravity-defying blunders of his life on Boxing Day, yet remarkably they didn't begin to disturb his momentum. The first, four from home, would have put most horses on the floor. Not this one. He stood off too far, changed his mind and put down, paddled through the fence and somehow survived. A moment later he cruised up to Racing Demon on the bend, led at the third last and was fully in command when he burst through the last fence as though it wasn't there. Once again Ruby Walsh sat tight before they sailed on to claim a famous victory. Exotic Dancer followed him in at a respectful distance of eight lengths.

Walsh was clearly baffled as he discussed Kauto Star's dramatic howlers. "I don't know why he does it," he admitted, shaking his head before adding. "Maybe it is a lack of concentration, but he has an unbelievable jump in him, yet after that mistake four out I was lucky to still be in the race. It was just about as bad a mistake as you can make but he still got himself out of it. It takes some technique for a horse to do that. Then halfway round the bend I thought, 'I'm still going to win.'

Nicholls suspected that the horse might have been distracted by the big TV screen and the vast crowd as he approached the last fence. For Clive Smith the experience of watching his brilliantly gifted horse threaten to throw it all away was proving hard to bear. "My heart was beating so much it nearly exploded. Some of his jumping wasn't great but he seemed to be able to plough his way through," he concluded.

As Kauto Star's team celebrated late into the afternoon at Kempton the Betfair bonus was never far from their thoughts. One more success in March and £1,000,000 was heading their way, the vast majority of it to Clive Smith. You couldn't ask for a better way to approach the New Year. The safest option would have been to send Kauto Star straight to Cheltenham, but Nicholls felt he would benefit from another race in the lead up to the Festival. The one he chose was the Grade 2 Aon Chase over three miles at Newbury on 10 February, a trial he had farmed in the past with See More Business, Valley Henry and Shotgun Willy.

He won it again this time with Kauto Star, but this was far from the relaxed dress rehearsal that many had anticipated. Instead he only just prevailed in a desperately tight finish after an alarming attempt at a one-horse demolition job on the last fence. He has long been a horse who can throw in the occasional blunder of earthquake proportions. It happened again as Tony McCoy launched the fiercest of challenges on the French raider L'Ami.

Perhaps flustered by the appearance of another horse beside him, Kauto Star reacted like a bungling novice by charging perilously into the fence with both knees. It was more than enough to put him on the floor, but an instinct born of survival somehow once again helped him stay on his feet when it seemed that he must turn over. Horse and rider emerged intact, but vital momentum had been lost and there was precious little time to recover.

All season we had marvelled at the sight of Kauto Star coasting imperiously to victory. Now suddenly he had to scrap for his life, to dig deeper than ever before like a champion boxer undone by a haymaker on the chin in the final round. What followed provided compelling evidence that this extraordinary horse possessed the steel and raw courage to go with the other splendid qualities that set him apart. It helped that in the saddle he had a jockey who understood the urgency of the moment. Beside them McCoy and L'Ami were in full flight but, in the nick of time, Walsh and Kauto Star were matching them stride for stride. It was uncomfortably tight for those who had supported the favourite at odds of 2-9, but at the line he had the verdict by a neck.

Afterwards Ruby Walsh was visibly shaken as he discussed the moment when his world threatened to turn upside down. "To me it felt like he was trying to bank the fence, and he's making a habit of it. That's as bad a mistake as he's made all season, and it happened so quick. He kept his back end so low and kicked through the fence with his front legs so that he wasn't going to fall.

"For a split second I thought, 'Shit, I'm gone.' He wasn't going to come down but I was going to come off him. You are never really ready for it. I thought going to the last fence he was going to jump it fine just as he had jumped all the others before it," he added, concern evident on his drawn features.

What worried him most was that Kauto Star wasn't giving him the slightest indication of when he was going to miss out a fence. "But at least he is staying on his feet when he does it. Tired horses fall, and he usually has so much in hand. When horses are about to empty they can't find a leg when they blunder. Ones with loads in the tank will usually find a leg. Kauto Star is so well balanced. When he makes a mistake he keeps his rear end low and his tail never gets up in the air.

"He's just a freak. After busting the last fence he stuck his neck out and ran on strongly. He likes a scrap, doesn't lie down easily. He wanted it as much as me and was brilliant apart from that one mistake, though he never switched off through the race."

Nicholls' frustration at this latest in a series of blunders was understandable. "We've almost come to expect it to happen now," he said. "I don't know why he keeps doing it and can't understand what goes through his head. He has run almost twenty times so he should know what he is going to do. It's almost as if he tries to hurdle or bank the last fence because he's racing at the time."

While Clive Smith expressed his confidence that his trainer and jockey could sort out the problem between them, there were sleepless nights ahead in the weeks leading up to the Gold Cup for all those close to Kauto Star. Here was a horse unbeaten that season in five starts at the highest level, yet the build-up to the Festival was dominated by a prolonged public debate about his jumping frailties. Nicholls found himself on the back foot, for once, defending his champion in a series of interviews.

He concedes, "It was getting to me that everyone was focusing on the issue of his mistakes. I felt all this talk was being too negative. All right, he'd missed a few fences, but he was still winning. It annoyed me that people kept saying he was a bad jumper because most of the time he was brilliant at his fences – the best."

Encouraged by some lengthy video reviewing of Kauto Star's races, and by a visit to Cheltenham where he walked the Gold Cup course, the trainer became increasingly confident that there would not be a repeat of his last-fence dramas on the big day. But how could punters be so sure it wouldn't happen again? He was more than ready for the question.

"After watching all those tapes I've worked out what Kauto does. It is always the same. When he comes under pressure he hangs left and looks for the rail. He did it first time in this country at Newbury as a novice. It is just the way he is and it gets him into trouble. Being a right-handed track, Kempton was probably the wrong way round for him. And at Newbury last time he was again wanting to go left and Ruby was trying to pull him right-handed to avoid the water jump looming up after the last fence.

"That's why they got in a muddle, but once the horse picked up the false rail half-way up the run in he was away again. Now we know what the problem is we can deal with it, and having walked round Cheltenham last week I'm confident that the nature of the course will be perfect for him. There is a rail on the inside all the way round and I'll be asking Ruby to stay tight on it," he said.

Kauto Star attempts to demolish the last fence at Newbury but still manages to win the Aon Chase by a neck from L'Ami, February 2007. No wonder Ruby Walsh said "I don't know why he keeps doing it..."

Nicholls was equally upbeat about Kauto Star's ability to stay the extra distance of the Gold Cup. "Everyone goes on about the trip but Clifford and I have no doubts about his stamina. Ruby couldn't pull him up at Haydock and he was hardly stopping at the end of three miles at Kempton. The key to the Gold Cup is his relaxing and switching off. I'm glad it is the last day for Ruby and me. That will ease the pressure. Ruby can get a bit wound up and is often better on the last day than the first. Hopefully he will have had a winner by then," he said.

Early in Festival week Clive Smith took part in a lively press conference laid on by Betfair in the tented area of the racecourse ahead of what was shaping up to be jump racing's biggest pay day. Pressed about Kauto Star's alarming tendency to throw in a clumsy jump at the business end of his races, Smith suggested, "It comes when he's at full stretch, being geed along, and I just wonder about the vibes from Ruby. There must be a certain vibe between the jockey and the horse and I just hope Ruby is cool with him," he said, before clarifying his remarks by adding, "Ruby is the best. He's fantastic. I'm looking forward to him riding the horse."

The jockey reiterated his long-held belief that Kauto Star was a 'once-in-a-lifetime' horse. "I can't wait to ride in the race and to find out whether he is good enough. You always want to be associated with great horses, and this fellow has been brilliant all season," he said. From a family steeped in racing history he reeled off the names of three enduring partnerships that are part of chasing folklore – Pat Taaffe and Arkle, Charlie Swan and Istabraq, and Jim Culloty and Best Mate.

He spoke too, of Kauto Star's infuriating mistakes and his athletic ability to survive them. "He's the best horse and I think he will jump round. If you look at his record you'll see that when he fouls up it's happened when he has had room to go left at the final fence, but he's become clever at surviving his mistakes, by keeping his hind legs down low. And he doesn't pitch on his head, that's the key. He keeps his back end down and gets his legs out preparing to land," he explained.

Walsh preferred to concentrate on Kauto Star's many fine qualities. He would ride his race with a plan firmly in mind, setting off in mid-field, hoping to stay close to the inside running rail before making his move once the cavalcade had spun left-handed on the final bend towards the two remaining fences. The problems posed by the last fence could take care of themselves.

Conditions at Cheltenham on Friday 16 March could hardly have been any better for a Coronation. The day was reasonably warm for the time of year, and crucially the ground had dried up markedly to the point where it was almost good in places. The field of eighteen that turned out for the Totesport Gold Cup was one of the biggest for many years, though it was definitely a case of quantity rather than quality, with only a handful of horses having any logical chance of upsetting Kauto Star, a rock-solid favourite at 5-4. Crucially the first two home twelve months previously, War of Attrition and Hedgehunter, were missing.

The stage was set for a new champion to emerge at the home of steeple-chasing, and if the frantic betting activity in the packed ring was any guide then Kauto Star was the overwhelming choice of most punters to be the one to rise to the top. Only two were seriously backed to beat him. Exotic Dancer, a 9-2 shot, ridden by the record-breaking champion jockey Tony McCoy, had sound claims, though the fact that he was again equipped with distinctive brown cheek pieces suggested he was not entirely straightforward. He'd finished eight lengths behind Kauto Star at Kempton and there was no obvious reason why he should reverse the form.

You could make a case of sorts for State of Play, an 8-1 chance, who had been kept fresh by his trainer Evan Williams since his decisive victory in the Hennessy Cognac Gold Cup. He had raced off a mark of 145 that day. Now he was taking on the best at levels, and you sensed his position as third favourite was mostly down to the paucity of the opposition. Short of breath-taking improvement over the winter it was hard to see how State of Play could topple the favourite.

For Paul Nicholls the biggest worry was the unexpectedly high number of runners, for the best-laid plans can be ended by a stricken rival or a faller taking others out as surely as a hidden trip wire. It has happened before in the Gold Cup. This time there were enough wild cards floating in the line-up to give Nicholls cause for concern. They included the French-trained pair Sybellius D'Artaix and Marble Garden, whose odds of 250-1 indicated that they had no business in a race of this importance. But the rules allowed it, so run they did.

So much was at stake as the field paraded in front of the stands. No one felt the pressure more than Nicholls, who finds watching his horses more an ordeal than a particularly enjoyable experience. Often he prefers to listen to the commentary rather than view the action, blow by blow. As

Kuato Star (Ruby Walsh in the purple cap) trails the leaders in the Cheltenham Gold Cup, March 2007.

the runners circled at the start he made himself scarce and found a convenient bolt hole away from prying eyes beside a little Tote kiosk adjacent to the paddock.

A few minutes later his belief in Kauto Star was gloriously justified as the horse delivered in the grand manner. For twenty-one fences he was immaculate, flowing through the race as if on autopilot, destiny beckoning. A surprisingly steady pace ensured that as many as ten horses were still in with a chance running downhill for the last time, though none was travelling as easily as the favourite, who moved stealthily into contention with Exotic Dancer on his quarters.

The choice for Walsh was to stay tight on the rail and risk being impeded as the tempo increased, or switch wide to find daylight. These decisions are made instinctively, in split seconds, by the best jockeys. One moment Kauto Star was locked away on the rail in danger of running into a traffic jam. The next his jockey angled him out and launched him on an irresistible charge on the crown of the bend.

Kauto Star ploughs through the last fence on his way to victory and overleaf, powers away from Exotic Dancer and Turpin Green as he gallops up the hill to the finish.

The response from Kauto Star will live long in the memory. He accelerated like a sprinter, passed seven or eight horses on his inside in less time than it takes to tell, and soared over the second last fence in front as if he had just joined in. It was a sight to stir the blood of all but the coldest of hearts. Then he did his best to spoil the script by tackling the last fence like a horse who was blind in one eye and couldn't see out of the other. Photographs published the next day showed just how close Kauto Star had been to disaster.

He started to edge left, lost concentration, got in closer than his jockey would have wished and sent the birch flying in all directions as he lurched into the fence like a bungling novice. It was a calamitous error which would have put nine horses out of ten on the floor and dislodged many jockeys. But normal rules do not apply to Kauto Star and Ruby Walsh who nimbly regained their balance and galloped on gaily up the hill to share a marvellous victory by two and a half lengths from Exotic Dancer. It was a breathtaking way to land the Betfair Million.

Horse and rider returned to sustained applause as they made their way back down the narrow chute in front of the massed ranks of racegoers packed into the stands. The cheering continued as they made their triumphant journey left-handed into the vast bowl at the end of the paddock which passes for the winners' enclosure. The Cheltenham faithful knew beyond doubt that they had just witnessed a performance that ranked alongside the best of the past two decades in the Gold Cup. As Kauto Star was only seven, with luck, there could be even better to come.

Paul Nicholls, Ruby Walsh and Clive Smith gave a series of brief interviews on the spot before giving more detailed analysis at the annual press conference conducted in a little marquee a few yards from the tote kiosk where the trainer had watched some of the drama unfold on a small television screen.

The relief on Nicholls' face was almost tangible as he spoke of the impact of this latest success by Kauto Star. "I've never had any doubt that this horse was the real deal, and maybe now you will believe he is a superstar. That wasn't bad for one who can't jump and doesn't stay. He was brilliant out there, and it was only a minor mistake at the last, where he had a lapse of concentration. It wasn't a real problem," he said, tongue firmly in cheek.

Nicholls could be forgiven for playing down the one flaw in a victory of exceptional merit. Why focus on that lone blunder when there was so much to praise? Later he would admit that he didn't watch much of the race, maybe just the last fence.

He explains: "I do prefer to be in my own little world when my horses are running. I saw little bits and pieces and could hear the commentary. Once I'd seen the video a couple of times I was shell-shocked at the way he won. He was awesome, quite amazing. I'd planned all year for this day and when it happened it was a bit overwhelming. I'm not knocking the others in the Gold Cup but in my book if Kauto Star stood up the others couldn't beat him.

"Yet before the race I kept hearing this rubbish with people slagging him off. I found that hard to take. It was definitely getting to me. I felt more pressure than ever before because he'd become a public horse, unbeaten all season, and all people seemed to do was pick holes in him. You do get annoyed listening to that sort of thing.

"OK, he'd had a few scares, but he never looked like falling all season and the mistakes were never going to stop him. You could hardly call him a bad jumper. I am a positive person. At times you stick your neck on the block and it gets cut off, but we always had belief in this horse and his jockey. They are made for each other."

Ruby Walsh spoke of the role played by Clifford Baker in teaching the horse to settle. "Even in the parade Clifford, who knows him better than anyone, told me that he had never known him so relaxed. That gave me even more confidence. Once I got him settled I knew it was a matter of when I wanted to press the button, though I was worried for a second when I pulled off the rail and saw A.P. go there on Exotic Dancer, but it was all OK in the end.

Gold Cup KAUTO STAR 2007

New champion. Kauto Star at home after his triumph at Cheltenham.

"We could not be certain of his stamina, but either they stay or they don't. He pinged two out and then it was time to go, a case of do or die. Kauto Star has come of age. He can be a bit leery in front but he was electric at his fences. To land the Betfair Chase, drop back in distance at Sandown, step up again in the King George and then go on to win the Gold Cup, well, I never thought I'd ride a horse that could do that. I never thought there would ever be a horse that could do that. He's phenomenal," he declared.

As he listened to his trainer and jockey, Clive Smith probably needed a calculator to work out all his winnings. His was a windfall unprecedented in the annals of steeplechasing. Take his early, lumpy bets on Kauto Star on Betfair, add the Gold Cup prize money of £242,335, throw in £750,000, his share of the Betfair Million, and he was suddenly richer by around £1.24 million. A few weeks later he would collect a further bonus of £200,000 after Kauto Star emerged as the clear winner of the Order of Merit.

For the second time in forty-eight hours Nicholls was pressed to nominate the day that his two outstanding chasers would clash for the first time. Once again he kept his cards unusually close to his chest about future plans,

115

though he gave a hint of his view on the outcome when they finally met as he suggested, "Cheltenham plays to Kauto Star's strengths and Denman will have to improve a bit to match him."

Nicholls made clear that both horses had finished for the season before adding that their daily workouts would gradually wind down in the coming weeks. He explained, "As they are finely tuned athletes you can't just switch them off. They came to Cheltenham like super-fit like boxers before a big fight. You can't stop the training sessions or they will fall apart. Ease up too quickly with them and they start behaving stupidly, especially Kauto Star."

The celebrations lasted long into the night at the Manor Inn at Ditcheat where gallons of pink champagne were consumed. Dawn was still a furlong away as Paul Nicholls crept downstairs, turned on his video and watched Kauto Star win the Gold Cup once more. The time was 5.30 and he'd managed barely four hours sleep. Now on his own, without the distraction of the telephone, he pressed the rewind button and had the chance to appreciate the fabulous quality of what had taken place the previous afternoon.

For Paul Barber, the joint owner of Denman, there was a chance to acknowledge the achievements of the trainer who had started his career in his converted dairy yard in 1991. What began as a diversification from farming years earlier had grown into a success story that had taken both men to the highest peaks of racing.

"Sometimes I pinch myself at the magnitude of it," admitted Barber over breakfast that morning. "Paul soon filled up all twenty-five boxes. Now there are horses everywhere and it has mushroomed to the point where his is the most powerful jumping yard in the land. It is astonishing. Paul is so positive he can't stop going forward. By sheer willpower he drives the whole thing along. Obviously I am excited by Denman but I think we are all waiting for Kauto Star to retire because I can't see anything beating him. He has the lot. The only time we might trouble him is in a slog on really soft ground over three and a quarter miles."

No one in racing was better placed to make the judgement. Later that morning Clive Smith arrived in time to join in the parade of Nicholls' champions through the streets of the village. The next day, before jetting off to Barbados for a well-deserved week's holiday, the trainer finally pencilled in his long-term plans for his two chasing superstars. Kauto Star would probably take in the Betfair Chase, the Tingle Creek and the King George VI Chase before a break, then one run in February ahead of the Gold Cup.

Denman would most likely return to action in the Hennessy Gold Cup before a trip to Ireland for the Lexus Chase at Leopardstown over Christmas. After that, he too would have time on the easy list before a prep race, most likely the Aon Chase at Newbury. Then he would be prepared for the Gold Cup. It was the first public acknowledgement that the clash the racing world craved would finally take place in March 2008.

In May the achievements of Nicholls and his blue-blooded team of horses were recognised at the Anglo-Irish Jump Racing Awards in London. Remarkably Kauto Star took five of the prizes as Horse of the Year, champion chaser at all distances, three miles plus, two and a half miles and two miles, and as winner of the Racing UK Order of Merit. No wonder Nicholls describes him as a 'once-in-a-lifetime' horse.

On the eve of Royal Ascot Clive Smith spent some of his winnings on an extravagant party at his own Pine Ridge golf club. Tables were decked out in Kauto Star's colours. So, too, was his owner, who sported a lively waistcoat in green and yellow spots beneath an immaculate tuxedo. After an evening of nostalgia with films, interviews and tributes Smith rolled back the years as he joined a hand-picked group of younger guests in an energetic Cossack dance.

The horse who launched all the celebrations spent the summer in his usual paddock at Highbridge with Denman, Twist Magic and Taranis.

Top team... The celebrations at the Anglo Irish Jump Racing Awards as Kauto Star is named Horse of the Year, May 2007.

117

CHAPTER 9

HEADING FOR A SHOWDOWN

Battle lines for the 2008 Tote Cheltenham Gold Cup were drawn at a startlingly early stage at Ditcheat, many months ahead of the ultimate test in March. As the title holder Kauto Star had the overwhelming backing of those who worked at Manor Farm stables. He was young, still improving, and with any luck at all the best was still to come. The world, as Arthur Daley used to say, was his lobster!

Denman had his supporters, too. They believed that he was capable of toppling his stable companion if the Gold Cup was run at a sufficiently searching pace to make it a thorough test of stamina. It was a view immediately enhanced by an unexpected reverse for Kauto Star on his return to action at Aintree at the end of October.

Paul Nicholls had spotted the warning signs during an unimpressive schooling session by his champion earlier in the week. Usually he devours the fences put in front of him. On this occasion, ridden by Ruby Walsh, he was uncharacteristically lazy, almost disinterested, as he fiddled his way round the indoor school, as if he had other things on his mind.

The trainer was sufficiently concerned to invite Sam Thomas to Ditcheat for a further schooling session on the Gold Cup winner on Thursday, two days before Aintree. This time he was much better, though Nicholls warned readers of the *Racing Post* that it would require an amazing performance if Kauto Star was to win the Old Roan Chase again. He felt he was bound to improve for the run, and this time, crucially, he was set to concede a stone to the smart grey Monet's Garden, and 7lb to his old rival Exotic Dancer.

Exotic Dancer ran a shocker, and when Ashley Brook came down heavily in front four out Monet's Garden was left with a handy lead which he was never going to relinquish. The writing had been on the wall from an early stage for Kauto Star, who was being vigorously chased along by Ruby Walsh at halfway. Usually he eases through his races in eye-catching style. Not at Aintree where, worryingly, for the first time, his jockey was having to bustle him along to keep involved.

Perhaps he was rusty. Maybe he was having an off day or it was simply a case of being unable to concede a stone to a talented horse who is usually at his best first time out. Whatever the reason this reverse was a rare blemish on Kauto Star's outstanding CV. He laboured throughout and was already beaten when he jumped markedly left at the second last before keeping on doggedly for second place one and a half lengths behind Monet's Garden.

Nicholls accurately described the performance as lethargic. "Most of all I was concerned that he raced lazily through the middle of the race, which is so unlike him. That did puzzle me. He wasn't his usual, normal buzzy self. But the bare form was good and I was encouraged by the way he was staying on strongly at the end. Remember he was dropping back six furlongs in trip from the Gold Cup," he said.

At the back of his mind was the mystery of another of his outstanding chasers, Call Equiname, whose form tailed off so alarmingly after he prevailed in the 1999 Queen Mother Champion Chase that he was retired without winning another race.

"That Cheltenham win definitely bottomed Call Equiname and I just hoped it wasn't the same with Kauto Star. It was unlike him to be so quiet, and if you didn't know otherwise you'd have sworn someone had given him half a pill before the race. Something had taken the edge off him," he recalls.

After considerable thought and a long chat with Clifford Baker the trainer decided on a change of routine for Kauto Star. Up to that point he had always been asked to gallop with the quickest horses in the yard. Now, in an attempt to rekindle his enthusiasm, he pitted him against some of the lesser lights at Ditcheat.

He explains, "I had this feeling that he was doing a bit too much in the mornings. Working with the lesser ones was a way of freshening him up."

Nicholls' plans for his two stable stars were thrown into confusion by a serious shoulder injury sustained by Ruby Walsh in a dreadful fall at Cheltenham on 17 November. At a stroke it left him without his outstanding stable jockey on the eve of vital races for both Kauto Star and Denman.

No one could be certain how long Walsh would be on the sidelines after dislocating his shoulder in a fall that claimed the life of his mount, Willyanwoody. His misfortune appeared to leave his deputy, Sam Thomas, in the hot seat, though in the following days there was speculation that other, more experienced jockeys might be in line for the ride on Kauto Star in the Betfair Chase at Haydock. Clive Smith considered turning to Mick Fitzgerald, but Nicholls moved swiftly to end further debate by announcing that Thomas would partner Kauto Star and also Denman a week later in the Hennessy Cognac Gold Cup. The soft-spoken teacher's son was firmly back in the frame.

Nicholls explains, "We'd taken on Sam as second jockey and it was going to mess things up if we didn't use him once Ruby was injured. I had every faith in him, he'd been schooling Kauto Star and the others and so I was happy to stand my ground. To be fair to Clive we had a conversation and he sided with me."

At Haydock Nicholls impressed on his young jockey that he had his full confidence and he should be in no doubt that he was on the best horse. If he was going well on Kauto Star along the back straight he should be prepared to seize the initiative. He also warned Thomas that the horse could idle in front. Walsh played his part by giving his deputy some sound advice on tactics.

For Clive Smith there was the niggling doubt that his horse had not brought his A game to Aintree. He reasoned, "There is the danger that he had a hard race by straining to win, though Paul assured me he would travel much better this time. Had six punishing races at the highest level the previous season left their mark? It was possible. This next run would tell us.

"I realised what everyone would say if he came in third and didn't run up to his best. Then again if he stormed home like twelve months previously it would be fantastic, a case of here we go again. I was quite philosophical about it. By that stage as a racehorse owner I felt I'd paid my dues and was used to the knocks in the game."

Clive Smith and his trainer were in jubilant mood after Kauto Star bounced back to form by beating Exotic Dancer on testing ground in the Betfair Chase. The plan had been for Sam Thomas to ride a waiting race but the suicidal early pace set by Ollie Magern demanded a change of tactics. It came when Thomas allowed Kauto Star to edge into the lead at the twelfth fence as Ollie Magern dropped away exhausted. He stayed there to the end, apparently in command, and although awkward at the last still had enough in reserve to resist the persistent charge of Exotic Dancer by half a length.

Nicholls told waiting reporters, "He is back on track, not that we were ever off track! I wasn't disappointed by what happened at Aintree. It was everybody else. I said all along that Aintree was a stepping stone for him. Today was always the target. Sam couldn't have ridden him better and we are back where we want to be with Kauto Star, which is a relief."

Thomas spoke of the race as a milestone in his career. He said, "Kauto Star was absolutely awesome and in a different class. It was a pleasure to ride him. He has done it the hard way, chasing Ollie Magern, and he ran all the way to the line when Exotic Dancer threatened."

Next it was the turn of Kauto Star's imposing neighbour to throw his hat into the ring. For months Harry Findlay had been keen for Denman to target the Hennessy, one of the most competitive chasing handicaps of the year at Newbury. When he raised the subject with Paul Nicholls early in the summer he was delighted to discover that his trainer was thinking along the same lines. The oldest surviving sponsored jumps race, first staged in 1957, the Hennessy has long been one of Nicholls' favourite races. He rode the winner in successive years in 1986 and 1987 on Broadheath and Playschool and had also won it as a trainer with the immensely talented Strong Flow in 2003.

Denman, he felt, was ideal for the Hennessy, which has frequently been dominated by second-season novices. Yes, he would have to carry top weight, but of all the horses that have been in his care none was better equipped to shoulder the considerable burden of 11st 12lb. Of more concern was the horse's fitness in the run-up to the race.

Nicholls will tell you Denman is so stuffy it takes an enormous amount of work to bring him to race fitness. That autumn, more than in previous years, it took an age for the weight to come off. Eight days before the Hennessy he sent Denman to Exeter for a public workout to help put an edge on his preparation. The big horse with the big following briefly threatened to down tools with Sam Thomas before breezing round a circuit of the track upsides the talented hurdler Desert Quest, partnered by Liam Heard. This was far from a proper gallop, more an attempt to blow away the cobwebs after a long break.

For such a positive man Nicholls was unusually downbeat about Denman's chances in the final days before the Hennessy. In a series of interviews he warned punters that the horse might need the run and that he faced a stiff task on a handicap mark of 161, giving as much as a stone and twelve pounds to some of the runners. He also pointed out that only three horses had won the race off a higher mark in the previous thirty-five years. Crucially, two of them, Burrough Hill Lad and Bregawn, were Gold Cup winners.

He explains "I just thought it was a big ask for a gross horse first time out after an absence of eight months. Frankly he faced a massive task. We do get them very fit at home and I hoped he'd go close, but that season we'd already seen Kauto Star and the two-mile champion Voy Por Ustedes beaten under top weight in handicaps. What I had in mind was that this run would put him right for his mid-winter target, the Lexus Chase at Leopardstown."

So much for inside information! The rampaging triumph of Denman at Newbury immediately set up a rip-roaring blood-and-thunder collision of the giants in the Tote Cheltenham Gold Cup in March. Ladbrokes couldn't split the pair at 2-1. For the moment, at least, Kauto Star remained the title holder, but Denman looked a lethal contender as he stormed to a runaway victory.

Harry Findlay couldn't disguise his excitement as he declared, "Everyone in racing wants to see these two clash. Let's get it on. OK, Kauto won it this year so he is still the champ. But everything will be in our favour next March and if it comes up soft or heavy on the day I think Denman's a certainty."

Never one to hide his light under a bushel, Findlay could be forgiven his bullish predictions after witnessing his horse demolish a high-class field of handicappers from the front with murderously intimidating ease. Dan Skelton was on guard at the start, as usual, just in case Denman misbehaved. This time he jumped off without a hint of trouble and settled better than expected. Yet he still showed in front after a mile, held a decisive lead on the final bend and charged home with the rest scampering for a place in his slipstream. Dream Alliance, in receipt of 19lb, took second place, fully eleven lengths back, with Character Building, receiving 26lb, plugging on for third.

Paul Nicholls thus became the first man to ride and train two winners of this great old race. He admits he watched the drama unfold with a mixture of pride and disbelief before making it clear his two heavyweights would not be pitched against each other until Cheltenham.

"We'll definitely keep them apart until then," he confirmed. "This is a great day, following on Kauto Star's success a week ago. The gap between them is going to close. There's no point in guessing now but at some stage Ruby Walsh is going to have to be man enough to pick between them," he suggested.

At the season's close he would look back at that milestone in Denman's career with a degree of nostalgia. "By then you could say he had two stone in hand at Newbury, that off 161 he had plenty in hand. I'd done as much as I could with him at home but knew there was a lot more to come from him. Before the race I said what I thought. He's such a huge horse, and was still a few kilos over his ideal racing weight, so how could I forecast that he'd definitely win first time up? Denman did surprise me and obviously I got it wrong. At that stage I didn't quite appreciate how good he was, but he was improving every day and the key to him at Newbury was that he settled for Sam Thomas in the first mile."

The following week Nicholls reported that Denman gave a few coughs on his return from Newbury, but he was due a couple of days on the easy list and was soon back in full training for his next appointment in Ireland on 28 December.

The sight of Kauto Star and Denman winning on successive Saturdays sharpened Ruby Walsh's resolve to recover in time to ride the pair over Christmas. Injured jump jockeys tend to take a masochistic pride in attempting to defy medical opinion by riding again much sooner than is advisable. In the

Harry Findlay and Sam Thomas celebrate Denman's storming victory in the 2007 Hennessy Gold Cup, Newbury, December 2007.

past, when their wounds and fractures were not so well documented, they would proffer a good arm or a sound leg to a doctor for examination when it was the other one that was damaged. Gerry Scott, later an outstanding starter, famously rode to victory on Merryman II in the 1960 Grand National, despite breaking his collarbone eight days earlier.

It couldn't happen now. Walsh took a short holiday in Hong Kong early in December before continuing his fitness programme. Next came a crucial consultation with his surgeon, Bill Quinlan, who gave the jockey the all-clear to resume at Thurles the weekend before Christmas. Then it was a case of

Kauto Star wins the 2007 King George VI Chase at Kempton for the second time at Christmas 2007.

twisting the arm of Paul Nicholls to allow him to take his place on Kauto Star at Kempton and Denman at Leopardstown two days later.

The champion trainer doubted that his jockey was ready for two such important rides so soon after his comeback. In his time in the saddle Nicholls had, at times, hoodwinked doctors and trainers in his desire to rush back with indecent haste for the next good race. Now, he suspected, Walsh was doing exactly the same, but he was hardly in a position to force him to stand down.

Nicholls confirms, "I was far from convinced that Ruby was fully fit, but he'd passed the doctor so what could I do? In his shoes I'd have done exactly the same."

Walsh, for his part, could reason that he had survived his comeback over hurdles at Thurles without any ill-effects and that he'd been riding out for his father and for Willie Mullins for much of that week. For him there was no argument. He was anxious to make up for lost time and, you sensed, would have walked a mile on broken glass to make his appointment with Kauto Star. His shoulder was immediately put to the test on his first ride of the afternoon at Kempton by Silverburn who pulled like a bone-headed mule for more than two miles before dropping tamely away in the closing stages.

Just over an hour later it was the turn of Kauto Star, a raging hot favourite at 4-6, to claim the King George VI Chase for the second time. In the paddock Nicholls urged his jockey to be positive. Exotic Dancer, beaten by only half a length at Haydock the previous month, was backed at 9-2 to turn the tables. This time it was plain sailing for Kauto Star, who eased into the lead five fences from home absolutely running away, readily pulled clear and popped safely over the last fence without a hint of drama.

Behind him the rest of the field appeared to be running on a platform of quicksand. Our Vic, an 11-1 shot, eventually won the battle for second place eleven lengths behind the hugely impressive winner. For Ruby Walsh it was the perfect Christmas present, fitting reward for his determination to return in time for this ride above all.

With Kauto Star now rated a 6-4 chance to retain his crown, Betfair's accountants were already preparing to fork out a second successive £1m bonus to Clive Smith and his team in March. Their only hope of salvation appeared to be housed in the box next to Kauto Star. Denman flew from Bristol to Ireland on 27 December with Jess Allen and former trainer Robert Baker in attendance. Baker experienced a moment of anxiety when the horse walked calmly from the loading ramp through the door of the cargo plane, a four-engined BAE 146.

He relates: "It was not a big door, and as Denman stepped through there were barely four inches clearance above his head. Once inside his stall he put his head up and his ears touched the roof of the fuselage. Realising that he couldn't do that again he put his head down and was as good as gold during the flight, a real gentleman. He just showed the whites of his eyes as we accelerated down the runway."

Three more challengers from this side of the Irish Sea travelled over for the Grade 1 Lexus Chase. With only two horses representing the host nation Denman was the centre of attention in the build-up to the race. Although he didn't eat up overnight at the racecourse stables at Leopardstown, he wolfed down his breakfast before being led out by Jess Allen to stretch his legs.

The task facing Denman was accurately reflected in his starting price of 4-9. On the form of his Hennessy victory nothing could touch him, but he was playing away, after an unfamiliar flight and a tiring journey. It was a bit like Chelsea taking on a lower league team away from home in the FA Cup. The result should be a formality but in sport, as in life, you can never be sure.

Opposite: Ruby Walsh and Denman are congratulated by Paul Carberry on Beef or Salmon after their win in the Lexus Chase, December 2007.

Denman proved more than equal to the task. He led as early as the third fence, jumping boldly, and was briefly pressed by The Listener and Mossbank at the second last, before stretching clear again on the flat in a manner that suggested he could have gone round again. It was a highly professional display, without flaws, though the four-length verdict over Mossbank suggested that improvement would be needed if he was to trouble Kauto Star at Cheltenham. Denman's reward was a return journey, with The Listener, by lorry and ferry.

As the New Year dawned Kauto Star remained a solid favourite for the Gold Cup, with Denman apparently the only credible danger. One man who had no doubt of the outcome was Paul Barber. Over breakfast in his conservatory one morning in January he offered the startling opinion that Denman would annihilate Kauto Star at Cheltenham.

"But something will probably come past the pair of them", he added with a warm smile. "If you watch Denman's races carefully you will see that when another horse comes to take him on he runs across the track to intimidate him and say 'bugger off'. That's what he does. It happened when he was challenged by Don't Push It at Cheltenham as a novice. That is why I think he will win the Gold Cup. There is something about him. As you saw in the

Hennessy no horse could have passed him even if they had jumped in to start half-way down the straight."

What did concern Barber was the identity of the jockey who would ride Denman in the Gold Cup. Barber will tell you that any decision is better than none. Now he and Findlay wanted a decision from Ruby Walsh ahead of the Aon Chase early in February at Newbury, which would be Denman's final race before the Festival. He explains: "It was tough on Ruby but Harry and I felt it was important that whoever rode him at Cheltenham should also be on him at Newbury."

Though Barber and Findlay were clinging to the hope that Ruby Walsh would pick Denman they were acutely aware that he was unlikely to desert the horse who had won the 2007 Gold Cup. In addition the jockey would be giving up the chance of his share of the Betfair Million if he switched to Denman.

After several days of debate Ruby Walsh announced on 5 February that he had sided with Kauto Star. "At the end of the day how do you get off a Gold Cup winner," he explained before adding, "It wasn't easy to choose between two great horses that have never run against each other. You have to remember Paul Barber played a big part in my riding for Paul Nicholls, which made my decision even harder. He was very understanding about it when I rang him."

Sam Thomas, once listed for a Bachelor of the Year award by a glossy magazine, was much happier to be appointed the ideal suitor for Denman, who set off as 1-4 favourite in the Aon Chase with Ruby Walsh in opposition for once on Regal Heights, trained by Donald McCain. From his remote vantage point on the back of Regal Heights Walsh surely had cause to question his Gold Cup decision as the horse he rejected stormed imperiously round Newbury in a totally different league to his three rivals. He did clout the cross fence on the second circuit but the race was as good as over by then and though eased long before the end he sped home twenty lengths clear of Regal Heights. It was a trial of savage authority.

Nicholls conceded, "That was just what was wanted and Sam said the horse was taking the mickey out of him the whole way. No one knows how good he is. He's having a right old blow and will improve a fair bit … but then he needs to."

Beside him Harry Findlay appeared to be winding himself up for another hefty ante-post investment on his pride and joy. "He's ready for a proper race now and he'll get it at the Festival. Kauto Star will win next week and I think it's great that these guys are in the same stable. Everything will be done right without malice. When they meet it will be a terrific advertisement for the sport. Yes, Denman certainly got one fence wrong, but that's the first error he's ever made. He's built like a tank, bulldozed it and tried to obliterate it, but it didn't stop him for a second or cost him any ground."

He then suggested, "In a fast-run Gold Cup there is a big chance that Kauto Star might not stay. We could beat him there and it would not necessarily make us a better horse. He is that good. The fact that the Gold Cup is at Cheltenham over three and a quarter miles is hugely in our favour. Back at three miles at Kempton I wouldn't expect Denman to get near him."

Findlay also revealed his long-term ambition to run Denman in the Grand National before conceding that it was unlikely to happen for at least two years. "I've never been more certain that a horse will win the National. The way he jumps and travels, he is made for it," he declared. "It helps that Phil Smith, the handicapper, is a massive fan of the horse and believes in giving top-class chasers a right good chance in the race."

Findlay's vaulting ambition, however fanciful, offered an interesting diversion from the serious business ahead in the 2008 Cheltenham Gold Cup. First, though, it was time for Kauto Star to steal the show on his final appearance before defending his crown. His flawless performance in the Commercial First Ascot Chase came as a timely response to the aggressive challenge laid down by his hulking stable companion at Newbury. Kauto Star was in front three out and readily saw off Monet's Garden by eight lengths.

Nicholls was disturbed to see his champion take a couple of false steps as he returned to the winner's enclosure. When he looked more closely the horse was 100% sound and there was not a sign of a problem as he was led away to the racecourse stables. The style of his victory seemed to justify the decision of Ruby Walsh to stay loyal to Kauto Star, though the jockey conceded matters would not be so straightforward in March. "The horse did everything we wanted him to do here. My decision has been made so there is no point wondering what is or what was. You just hope to God they both get there," he said.

Walsh's words proved to be uncannily prophetic. Barely two hours later Kauto Star's chances of defending his title appeared to be in the balance after he was found to be hopping lame behind. The alarm was raised by Sonia Warburton as she led him out of his box at the racecourse's stables towards the lorry waiting to take him to Ditcheat.

She recalls, "At first he wasn't too bad but after a few steps he was very lame, though he is such a wimp maybe he made it look worse than it was. The journey home that night was the longest of my life because no one knew for sure what was wrong with him."

Donna Blake, Nicholls' experienced travelling head girl, immediately alerted the trainer and summoned the racecourse vet, who, suspecting that the horse had twisted his off-hind joint, strapped up the damage and put it in a support dressing. The trainer's mobile was close to meltdown as he sought more information from the racecourse while repeatedly trying to contact Clive Smith without success. At the same time he was besieged by phone calls from news men alerted by an alarming drift in Kauto Star's Gold Cup odds on Betfair. As the story spread some bookies suspended betting on the race.

Ascot's vets wanted to keep the horse under observation overnight at the course before sending him to Newmarket for further examination. The only beacon of hope for Nicholls in a depressing scenario was the news that a series of X-rays had failed to show any kind of injury in the area of the fetlock joint. In addition the horse had been sound when he was led out by Sonia Warburton for a pick of grass an hour or so after his race. Armed with this information the trainer instructed Donna Blake to bring Kauto Star back to Ditcheat where he arranged for his own vet, Buffy Shirley-Beavan, to check him over first thing on Sunday. He then alerted the Press Association to say that he'd be making a statement on the horse's condition in the morning.

Nicholls explains: "I was clinging to the fact that Kauto Star was still sound an hour after the race so there had to be a chance he hadn't broken anything. After an age I tracked down Clive, told him what had happened and that we'd have another look at the horse once he was back in his own box. All sorts of dark thoughts were going through my mind as I waited with Clifford Baker and Paul Barber for him to arrive. I was sick with worry, but once Kauto Star stepped off the lorry shortly after nine I was relieved to see that he wasn't badly lame."

Time seemed to stand still as the horse was led into his box, where Baker removed the strapping from his joint, then gently eased off the shoe from the suspect leg. The canny head lad already suspected that the problem might be in his foot, and when Nicholls tried a pressure test on the foot Kauto Star jumped into the air as though he'd been stabbed in the ribs.

He remembers: "His foot was really warm to the touch, which gave us

hope that he was suffering from nothing worse than pus in his foot. Perhaps it had been brewing before Ascot. Having a race in that condition would have left him in serious discomfort. It was encouraging that he seemed much more comfortable once the shoe came off. If we were right then he should be fine in two or three days. If not …. It didn't bear thinking about. I didn't get a wink of sleep that night and was back in the yard long before first light, checking on his condition."

The crisis was over the moment Buffy Shirley-Beavan dug a small hole in Kauto Star's foot. Pus immediately came pouring out from the wound. The relief on the faces of those present was almost tangible. The vet poulticed the foot before suggesting that the patient could be led out for a short walk later in the morning. Remarkably he was sound by then and almost sound at the trot. His recovery was so swift that by Wednesday he was back cantering. Given what was at stake there would be many more sleepless nights for Paul Nicholls in the coming weeks. But for the moment at least the Gold Cup was back on the agenda.

Showdown: one of the most eagerly anticipated sporting rivalries of modern times. Ruby Walsh and Sam Thomas join in the hype.

CHAPTER 10

THE ENEMY WAS
NEXT DOOR

Battle was finally joined between Kauto Star and Denman at Cheltenham on Friday 14 March 2008. It seemed as though the entire nation paused in mid-afternoon to witness the historic showdown between the two stable companions. For those with a sense of history drawn back to this incomparable meeting each March this was the most eagerly awaited confrontation since Arkle put Mill House to the sword in 1964.

Ten others took part but you would hardly have known it as the build-up to the race reached a frenzied peak on the final day of the Festival. Many racegoers wore badges and scarves to mark their allegiance to the two protagonists who dominated the market in the betting ring. Kauto Star, considered the banker of the week by many punters, was a rock-solid favourite at a shade of odds on. Denman, whose remorseless power would strike fear into the heart of the doughtiest of champions, was heavily supported at 9-4. Exotic Dancer was next in the betting at 17-2 with Nicholls' third contender Neptune Collonges one of the outsiders at 25-1.

The champion trainer played an admirably straight bat to all inquiries, but on the eve of the race you sensed his deep-seated emotional ties to the title holder who had already given him so many days to remember. He agreed "Whatever beats Kauto will have to be a superstar. Denman might be that, but we can't be sure on what he's done so far. My take has always been that Kauto Star will be hard to beat. He is awesome and Denman is a potential champion. No one, not even me, knows if he is good enough for the step up to the next level. If he beats Kauto then, wow, without a doubt you will have seen a superstar performance.

"This clash is what everyone, including me, wants to see, though it is a shame one of them has to lose. Their meeting in the Gold Cup is great for the sport but I am finding the whole thing increasingly nerve-wracking. It is the biggest thing in my life, far beyond the normal spectacle at Cheltenham. So much is at stake.

"This season the two horses are head and shoulders above everything else and each jockey will be given orders that I think will maximise their particular chance of winning. Obviously Denman is going to be handy, but I've warned Paul and Harry that you can get a good stayer beaten in the Gold Cup by making too much use of him. With Kauto you never know how much he has left in the locker at the end of a race because he looks to do it all so easily. I can tell you it is not just a case of filling them up with petrol, turning the key and off you go. That doesn't happen. You can only have them at their very best on one or two days a year."

In his role as ringmaster Paul Nicholls gave his final instructions to his three jockeys, then retreated to the anonymity of the little Tote kiosk beside the paddock. He didn't watch all the action on the TV screen in front of him but he saw enough by half-way to convince him that a new name was about to be inscribed on the Gold Cup roll of honour.

Instead of the head-to-head duel we had all anticipated we found ourselves applauding a demolition as Denman, menacing, mean and magnificent, disembowelled the opposition. Sam Thomas had been content to track Mick Fitzgerald on Neptune Collonges for the first half of the race, and the writing was already on the wall as he allowed Denman to stretch on into the lead with a circuit to go. Behind them, to the dismay of his admirers, Kauto Star, hampered by sloppy jumping, was struggling to keep in touch.

Heading out into the country for the final time Denman began to draw clear, answering willingly each time his jockey heaped on the coal. Would Kauto Star be able to respond? Could he respond? Frankly he might as well have tried to catch the wind, for ahead of him Denman was powering on, a world-class heavyweight preparing to deliver the knock out blow.

Further mistakes, notably at the fourth from home, put an end to Kauto Star's chances, and long before the end Denman was running in a race of his own. He winged the last fence and set off up the hill like a war horse charging into the heat of battle. He had delivered a master class of old-fashioned jumping and galloping on the greatest stage that National Hunt racing can offer. Behind him, to his eternal credit, Kauto Star never gave up the chase and kept on dourly to claim second prize by a short head from Neptune Collonges.

For months we'd suspected that the enemy was next door. Now Denman had confirmed it in a thunderous manner which put an end to further argument just as Arkle had done all those years ago. Ruby Walsh's immediate reward for a valiant performance on Kauto Star was a robust smacker on the cheek from Sam Thomas.

At the top of the chute where the runners return Jess Allen was beside herself as she rushed to greet her favourite horse. "I screamed so loud and for so long at the finish people probably thought I should have been locked up," she admits with disarming candour. "Thank God the TV cameras were not on me."

In the chaos of the winner's enclosure Thomas delivered his own stylish version of a flying dismount. As racegoers stampeded through the enclosures to applaud the new champion, it would have required a vivid imagination for anyone to suggest that Kauto Star could ever turn the tables on his conqueror. Clive Smith, however, bravely kept the faith by declaring that his horse would set the record straight in twelve months time.

"We'll have him in the re-match", he declared defiantly. No one believed him at the time, but subsequent events would more than justify his testy response in the moment of defeat.

As the man who had just saddled the first three finishers in the 2008 Gold Cup, Paul Nicholls was fully entitled to give himself a huge pat on the back for a job well done in exceptionally trying circumstances. Yet he later admitted to a degree of shock at the defeat of Kauto Star, who never travelled through the race with his usual fluency. He said, "OK, he came off second best, but don't write him off. Denman was awesome. He looked the best he's ever been and got Kauto on the back foot by jumping and galloping. I'm not making excuses but for whatever reason Kauto wasn't sparking and didn't jump as he usually does. Horses are like people. You can't be at your best every day.

"Kauto Star was wound up in the racecourse stables walking round and round, and once he hit those two fences at the end of the first circuit I knew it was over for him. He wasn't cruising like he usually does. Down the hill I thought he might be beaten by twenty-five lengths and I was proud of the way he kept going to reduce the gap to seven lengths. That showed real character. He will be back."

Flying dismount... Sam Thomas leaps from the back of Denman, after winning the 2008 Cheltenham Gold Cup by seven lengths from Kauto Star.

Nicholls was clearly not in a hurry to arrange a re-match. "Maybe they will not meet again. Whatever happens we will probably try to keep them apart until next year's Gold Cup because the races that suit one don't necessarily suit the other, so there are hardly any opportunities for them to clash."

The trainer was keen to praise Sam Thomas before revealing that he had given him a well-deserved bollocking for an ill-judged ride in the race before the Gold Cup. He confirmed "Sam got a right cussing for his effort on The Tother One. I told him to put that out of his mind and concentrate on Denman. I thought his tactics were spot on."

Thomas admitted to being in a world of his own in the hours after the Gold Cup. "I am lost for words and still pinching myself. Denman was loving it out in front. The moment he landed over a fence he was looking for the next one," he said.

Paul Barber spoke of his admiration for the trainer whose drive and ambition had been evident from his first day at Ditcheat in 1991. "Paul has this whole-hearted enthusiasm that sweeps everyone along with him. Nothing is allowed to get in the way of his training the horses. In fact he talks about nothing but horses. If he went off to the Houses of Parliament all he would talk about is horses," he suggested.

Barber recalled his ambition in his early twenties to milk 1,000 cows and own the winner of the Cheltenham Gold Cup. "Now I milk 2,000 cows and Paul has given me my second Gold Cup," he declared.

Beside him in the press conference a croaky Harry Findlay, for once almost speechless after shouting Denman home, was fielding endless text messages on his two phones. Eventually he recovered his voice as he insisted, "Today is a carbon copy of the Hennessy. You get the lead, you go clear on the final circuit and you do the damage. Denman was very neat at his fences today. That's what won the race. The Tank blew them all away."

By now Findlay was moving into top gear as he observed, "If I owned another top horse I wouldn't go near Denman. Who will want to take him on next season?" The answer to that question would come back to haunt him twelve months later.

Phil Smith, the BHA's head of handicapping, offered an official assessment on a stunning result. He said "There can be no doubt Denman is up there with the likes of Desert Orchid and Burrough Hill Lad. Who knows how much improvement there is to come? I've raised him to 185 from 176 and kept Kauto Star on a rating of 180, though I suspect he ran 2lb below that," he said.

Later that evening the party moved on to the Manor Inn at Ditcheat where around thirty sat down to dinner, during which speeches were made to honour the rare feat of Paul Nicholls training the first three in the Gold Cup. The meal was at an end by the time Findlay and his entourage arrived to join in the fun. They had to make do with fish and chips.

Nicholls replayed the race on his video countless times that night before snatching a few hours' sleep. Early on Saturday morning in his office tears coursed down his face as he watched an outstanding reprise of the previous day's events on Channel 4's Morning Line. There were tears of joy at the sight of Denman exceeding his expectations. At the same time he was naturally upset, and surprised, at the way Kauto Star had been abruptly removed from his pedestal.

"Seeing Kauto Star well beaten by Denman was so hard for me. I didn't expect it and was gutted afterwards at the same time as being thrilled for Denman. Talk about mixed emotions," he said.

Back at his farm after four hectic days at Cheltenham, Paul Barber suggested that Denman had prevailed by taking Kauto Star out of his comfort zone. It was a view widely shared at the time. "Any horse that showed the speed Kauto has done over two and two and a half miles had to be a doubtful stayer. It was the only hole we could find in him and we had to try to exploit it," he explained.

That morning hostilities were set aside as Denman, Kauto Star and Neptune Collonges paraded through the village. Nicholls made it clear that Denman was finished for the season. The fact that the horse was steaming hot for two hours after the Gold Cup offered vivid testimony of the supreme effort he had put into winning. He eventually cooled down after Donna Blake washed him all over with cold water several times. Back in his box at Ditcheat he spent much of the time with his back to the door taking little interest in life in the yard. Usually he never lies down in his box. Yet when Dan Skelton checked round late at night during the rest of March he would often find Denman fast asleep on the floor.

Kauto Star, however, showed no ill-effects from his defeat at Cheltenham. He was bouncing within days, matching strides with Clive Smith's French recruit Master Minded, who had been the easiest winner of the Festival in the Queen Mother Champion Chase. At a meeting between trainer and owner it was decided that if ground conditions were suitable and Kauto Star continued to thrive at home they would send him to Aintree where a good run would seal another hefty bonus of £200,000 for topping in the Order of Merit for the second successive year.

"There's no reason not to run Kauto Star, who is giving me all the right signals. Believe me, if I could find half a reason why he shouldn't be running he wouldn't be," said Nicholls on the eve of Aintree. It was entirely reasonable to expect him to prevail in a small, select field for the Totesport Bowl Chase. Although the gap between the two races at Cheltenham and Aintree was only twenty days, that was hardly sufficient reason for Nicholls and Smith to turn their nose up at a purse of £91,000 for Kauto Star, who was guaranteed to start at long odds-on.

Yet a crucial change in tactics suggested by the trainer led to a dramatic defeat for Kauto Star and a rare disagreement with his jockey. Nicholls asked Ruby Walsh to try to put a seal on the race by pressing on into a clear lead early in the straight in much the way he had won at Kempton on Boxing Day. Walsh wasn't convinced about the need for change. He has long shown that he can ride any kind of race to suit his mounts, though, given the choice, he much prefers playing his cards late by smuggling his horses round in the rear, conserving energy, before delivering them when the leaders have had enough.

Perilous... Kauto Star bursts through the second last at Aintree before losing by a nose to Our Vic in April 2008.

Not this time. Conscious of his instructions he found himself involved in a duel for much of the final circuit with Tommy Murphy on the 9-1 shot Our Vic. The pair raced head to head with Our Vic just winning the exchanges until Kauto Star worked his way into a lead of five, perhaps six lengths after crossing the third last fence. Victory surely beckoned until he was left floundering after ploughing through the ditch, two out, as though it wasn't there. Suddenly he had a fight on his hands as Our Vic began to close. At the final fence Kauto Star still held the call by a length and a half but he was running on empty on the flat and was nailed on the line by Our Vic. The official verdict? A nose.

Aware that new tactics had brought about his downfall, Walsh was fuming as he returned to unsaddle, as much with himself as with the trainer. "I should have hung onto him. Normally I'd have the balls to do what I want," he declared, the pain of defeat clear in his eyes.

Nicholls took the criticism on the chin. "Ruby was mad at me and steaming. I was wrong on the day by telling him to try and sail on when he would have been better getting a lead. Kauto Star was then idling a bit in front, and it is a long run-in. Most times we get it right between us but I will take the blame here."

Later that afternoon he would add, "I think we know how to deal with each other. I might say something after a race and Ruby will snap my head off, then ring that night to say he should have done this or that. For the pair of us anything that gets beat is a low. The way we think, second is nowhere, and if Ruby believes he has given one of mine a bad ride he will say so."

That evening he suggested that Walsh should study the video of the race and then throw it away. He also texted him saying it was one of the worst rides he'd ever given one of his horses and that it was also one of his worst training performances. Walsh responded immediately, agreeing on both counts.

He explains, "When we have a difference of opinion it is a discussion more than anything else. I respect Paul and I think he respects me so we don't have rows as such. If we think something should be done we say so, but neither of us is looking to score points."

Nothing more needed to be said about Kauto Star's shock defeat at Aintree. The matter was as good as closed. The two men have shared no end of important big race successes, but even they can't get it right every time.

For Denman there was one more trick to play before a well-deserved holiday. Sent to Sandown to parade on the final day of the season with other equine stars, he broke lose from Jess Allen and displayed the pace of a five-furlong sprinter as he careered across the paddock towards the exit. Drama was only averted when the horse slowed to a halt and allowed himself to be caught by Dan Skelton.

It was the last act in a long partnership with Allen, who was giving up her job with Nicholls to have a baby in August. She recalls "Denman tugged me round the ring and probably thought he was going racing. Then he started rearing up and pulling away. The third time he did it he tore the lead rein out of my hands. He was so excited at breaking free he couldn't believe his luck, but he was probably loose for twenty seconds and no harm was done though I didn't relax until he was safely back in the horsebox. I knew I was going to miss him like mad because he'd given me some unbelievable days. It was lovely to be having a baby but it did shorten my time with Denman."

Kauto Star's long-time lass Sonia Warburton expressed regret, too, as she departed from Manor Farm Stables to plan her wedding the following year. She admits "It was very hard for me to give him away, but the real reason I left was because another of my horses, Thisthatandtother, was retiring. He meant more to me than Kauto Star because I'd looked after him for seven years. Mentally I'd had enough. I needed to get away from it all for a break."

That summer it was the turn of Paul Barber to host a party for Denman at Charlton House Hotel near Shepton Mallett. Guests including Sam Thomas and Clive Smith were treated to a champagne reception in the garden before lunch. Later there were speeches and an excellent cabaret by the singer Zoe Tyler, who had travelled from London. It was a memorable way to celebrate one of the outstanding steeplechasers of our times. And as the drink flowed late into the afternoon the conversation inevitably turned towards the next confrontation between Denman and Kauto Star.

On the loose... Denman leads Kauto Star in the parade of champions at Sandown, just before he breaks free from Jess Allen.

CHAPTER 11

A SPECTACLE FIT FOR THE QUEEN

The countdown to the 2009 Tote Cheltenham Gold Cup started unusually early for Paul Nicholls. Keeping the two outstanding candidates apart until March was not going to be a problem since he was the one making the decisions. Keeping them both in the best of health proved to be altogether more challenging, and all bets were off once Denman was diagnosed with a serious heart problem in September.

The alarm was raised by Nicholls' PA, Sarah West, who replaced Jess Allen on Denman that autumn. An accomplished point-to-point rider, she was thrilled to be offered the chance to sit on the big horse during first lot before attending to business in the office for the rest of the day. But her delight soon turned to disbelief at the sluggish manner of Denman's homework.

She explains, "I'd been so looking forward to riding this great horse and he gave me no feel at all. It was such a let down because he felt more like a slow hunter than a champion racehorse. He wasn't interested in picking up the bit and there was nothing I could do to make him go."

Lucinda Gould was concerned, too. She had taken over Denman that autumn in her second year at Ditcheat after graduating from Exeter University with a joint honours degree in German and classical music. "Not an ideal preparation for mucking out in the mornings," she giggles. "Denman was enormous when he came back in, then after a while started to lose weight quite rapidly. He wasn't eating well and was dull in his eye and coat."

Paul Nicholls called in Buffy Shirley-Beavan after he schooled without any zest with Sam Thomas in the middle of September. Normally Denman flows round the school, devouring his fences. Not this time. His jumping was laboured before the trainer swiftly brought an end to proceedings.

The next morning Shirley-Beavan checked Denman thoroughly before and after his regular morning canter. Her diagnosis came as a dreadful shock to Nicholls and everyone at Manor Farm Stables. Denman, she declared, was suffering from atrial fibrillation of the heart, which in layman's terms is a form of irregular heartbeat. Without treatment, she explained, his racing career was at an end.

The solution was to send him to a specialist cardiologist at Rossdales Veterinary Practice in Newmarket, who would try to return his heartbeat to normal. The procedure undoubtedly involved risk, but if it was successful there was a reasonable chance that he could race again as effectively as before. Nicholls drew encouragement from the knowledge that another of his horses, Eurotrek, had won two races after treatment for the same ailment.

Denman's heart problem came as an untimely blow to Lucinda Gould, who was only just getting to know him. As he set off for Newmarket on 22 September no one could be sure he would be returning in a few days' time. Celia Marr was the vet assigned to treat the Gold Cup winner at Newmarket. She explains that a fibrillating heart loses the co-ordination of a normal heartbeat.

"There are plenty of reasons why a heartbeat may be irregular, and two options to deal with it. Both can prove fatal. What we try to do with drugs or electricity is temporarily stop all the electrical activity in the heart for a milli-second. You are trusting that the heart's normal pacemaker will then take over and return back to normal. The quicker you pick up the problem the better, so it was encouraging to hear that there was no sign of a problem when Denman had a physical check-up in July," she added.

Marr chose to use Quinidine in powder form to treat Denman. This is given through a stomach tube at two-hourly intervals as the drug also acts as an extreme irritant and can cause colic and diarrhoea. If it is administered by mouth it causes unpleasant ulcers. In addition, the more of the drug you give, the worse the side effects. Throughout the process nurses monitor a horse's heartbeat for the good reason that if it is adversely affected the animal can die.

Fortunately for Denman the third dose of Quinidine had the desired effect so there was no need for the alternative, arguably more difficult option, which involves trying to kick-start the heart with electrical shocks. Technically this is much more challenging as it involves inserting electrodes directly into the heart so that the shock is given right in the heart muscle.

Marr recalls, "We tried the simple solution first and it worked, but Quinidine makes horses feel awful. We like to let them rest and recover before sending them home for a long recuperation."

The crisis was over for Denman but the long road to recovery would test the ingenuity of his trainer as never before. Back in his box in the care of Lucinda Gould he was weak and listless, and lacked energy, much like someone who has come through a serious operation. Just about all that he could manage most mornings was a leisurely stroll on a lead rein for a pick of grass. At that stage the Gold Cup seemed a million miles away.

Nicholls recalls: "I was warned that the drugs used to treat him would have much the same effect as chemotherapy on humans, and we had to nurse him along for quite a few weeks. He was just ticking over at best, gradually regaining some condition. There was no question of starting him back into regular work because he wasn't ready for it and you had to wonder if he would ever be as good again."

Lucinda Gould leads out Denman.

As the most famous equine patient in the country Denman was the subject of regular medical bulletins in the racing papers. While Paul Nicholls expressed his relief that he was continuing to show signs of a full recovery he made clear that it was far too soon to decide if he would be able to defend his crown in March.

Lucinda Gould explains: "He'd been through a horrible procedure and when he came back to Ditcheat he was really poorly, half the horse he had once been. It was hard to see him like that, but ever so slowly, with lots of nursing and TLC, he started to perk up."

While Denman remained on the sidelines Kauto Star bounced back with the most impressive success imaginable in the JNwine.com Champion Chase at Down Royal on 1 November. Any lingering doubts about the effect of two hard races ending in defeat at the end of the previous season were swept away by an exuberant display of jumping. The opposition was not the strongest, but Kauto Star, a 2-5 chance, could not have won more easily as he sauntered home twelve lengths ahead of Light on the Broom at the end of a breathless canter. The result was tangible confirmation that his homework had been of the highest class before he set off in midweek with his new lad, budding commentator Nick Child, for the long journey by road and ferry to Northern Ireland.

Master class... Kauto Star wins the JNWine. com Champion Chase at Down Royal in November 2008.

No one was happier at the result than Ruby Walsh, who was relieved to find his old comrade pulling his arms out once more. "Last season I was always

squeezing him along, even the day we won at Ascot. Today he took me along the whole way and didn't start to relax until the fourth last."

Clive Smith would not have passed the vet after arriving at the course on crutches nursing a broken ankle. He had slipped and fallen while attempting to jump the Swilcan Burn that crosses the fairway on the Old Course at St Andrews with his ball already on the first green. Perhaps he needed more schooling!

Bookmakers immediately trimmed the winner to as short as 4-6 for his hat-trick bid in the King George VI Chase. With his stable mate still under doctor's orders the way seemed clear for Kauto Star to reclaim his position at the top of chasing's tree. But nothing in this sport is ever straightforward, and another serious injury sustained by Ruby Walsh thirteen days later left Paul Nicholls facing a headache over riding arrangements that would have far-reaching consequences.

Walsh ended up in intensive care when he fell with Pride of Dulcote at Cheltenham. Doctors at Cheltenham General Hospital discovered that he had ruptured his spleen, was bleeding severely and his blood pressure was dropping at an alarming rate. They operated immediately to remove his spleen.

With Walsh on the sidelines Sam Thomas was again called up to replace him. This time, though, the dice did not roll his way. A series of falls put him under such immense pressure that he would eventually lose his high-profile job as second jockey to Paul Nicholls. The unhappy sequence began when he was unshipped by Kauto Star after the horse stumbled and pitched on landing at the last fence as he was bidding to claim the Betfair Chase for the third year running.

Kauto Star had already blundered three from home and though he may well have won but for his second error you couldn't be sure he would have beaten the winner Snoopy Loopy. Thomas, however, felt he would have prevailed. "He was finishing well and I'm absolutely gutted. Words can't describe it but thankfully the horse is OK," he said.

Paul Nicholls suspected that the decision to scrap Haydock's splendid old fences and replace them with portables set on the inside of the track had not played to Kauto Star's strengths. "It is a speed course now and he's a stayer," he explained before adding that the race might have come too soon after the horse's tiring journey to Northern Ireland.

"Perhaps that took more out of him than we realised at the time and it may be that he is best with his races spaced out. That might be the way for him in the future," he forecast.

The next day at Aintree Thomas was again picking himself up after being sent spectacularly into orbit by Gwanako at the Chair fence. Further tumbles, most notably from Big Bucks at the last fence in the Hennessy Gold Cup, led to a request from Clive Smith that Tony McCoy should partner his brilliant two-mile champion Master Minded at Sandown early in December. All jockeys experience bad runs when confidence drops, winners are elusive and the world seems to be against them. By this stage Thomas was urgently in need of a pick-me-up and he got it when Nicholls kept the faith by booking him for Noland, who won a Grade 1 Chase in Ireland three days later.

Parting of the ways for Kauto Star and Sam Thomas at Haydock, November 2008.

Smith was already beginning to fret about a jockey for Kauto Star's hat-trick bid at Kempton. So he was delighted and relieved in equal measure to hear the astonishing news that Ruby Walsh was eager and ready to resume two weeks before Christmas. It is doubtful if any top-class sportsman whose spleen has been removed has returned to action more quickly than Ruby Walsh. Some have taken up to six months to recover their core strength before competing again at the highest level. Yet Walsh has always been an exceptionally fast healer and in Dr Adrian McGoldrick, chief medical officer with the Turf Club, he has the soundest of allies.

When Nicholls called to see Walsh the afternoon following the fall he was astonished to discover that he had already been walking regularly round his hospital ward. Even then the patient, wrapped in a dressing gown, was confident that he would be back within four or five weeks, certainly in time for Kempton, and he continued to work on his fitness when he returned to Ireland after six days.

The next morning he twice walked half a mile to his local shop and back. "And when my own GP came to see me on the Sunday I could see he was expecting me to be in bed. Instead I was waiting for him in the sitting room and he was very surprised to see how quickly my operation scar had healed," he told me at the time.

"There is very little fat on me and the incision was only through the gristle between the two muscles. I told my GP I was aiming to resume on Master Minded in a fortnight, though maybe that was stretching things too far. It just depended on how quickly I progressed. He told me I was stupid, that the timing wasn't realistic. But I assured him if I continued to improve as I had done up to then that was the date I was aiming for."

Walsh's own specialist and Dr McGoldrick were both optimistic of his making an early return after giving him a thorough examination. McGoldrick confirmed, "When I saw Ruby nine days after his operation you would have thought it had taken place a month previously. He had healed much quicker than an ordinary person from similar surgery. It was all down to his fitness levels and diet and showed that he is an elite athlete."

You sense that if the jockey had been allowed to have his way he would have somehow levered himself onto the back of Master Minded at Sandown on 6 December. But thankfully common sense prevailed. McGoldrick, sage and experienced, persuaded Walsh to wait an extra week before resuming at Cheltenham on Friday 12 December, twenty-seven days after his fall. This gave him precious extra time to test his strength by riding out again for his father and Willie Mullins.

Walsh was eager to play down suggestions he was putting himself at risk by rushing back to his perilous trade. "You can only do what your body lets you, and my body is fine. There is not a bother on me. After a week I knew I'd be riding again well before Christmas. I didn't really have to persuade my specialist because he could see I was 100%," he said.

While Nicholls was thrilled to have his friend back so soon he was also anxious to help him play himself back into form without taking unnecessary risks. He restricted him to one mount, Mahonia, over hurdles on that first day back and tried to hand-pick his rides in the run up to Christmas.

He confirms: "I felt we had to mind Ruby over the next ten days, a bit like a young horse who needed looking after, with the idea that he would be at his peak again on Boxing Day. He came to Ditcheat more often than usual in that period, which was a bonus for me because we are really good mates too, and he is great company. Gradually I could see his confidence returning, and when he won two races for me at Fontwell on 23 December I knew he was as good as ever."

Clive Smith was invited to join the panel of experts on Channel 4's Morning Line live from Kempton on Boxing Day. He arrived in good humour, full of confidence, though he was briefly lost for words when the programme's resident windbag John McCririck asked him if he would be retiring Kauto Star if he didn't win that afternoon. Smith, sensible fellow, chose to let his horse do the talking.

You would never have known Ruby Walsh had been away as he and Kauto Star shared a barn-storming third triumph in the King George VI Chase. His odds of 10-11 looked a gift as he surged relentlessly clear in the final straight on his way to logging a searingly fast time.

Walsh declared, "He is a star, isn't he? The pace was strong, he put in a few good jumps and just ran away from them. He's always been a wonderful horse and you'd love to own him."

Paul Nicholls was already looking forward to a fourth King George as he offered an uncharacteristically belligerent defence of his great champion. "Some of the things people have been saying about him have been out of order. They have been slagging him off unfairly after three defeats in four runs. I just wish people would give him the respect he deserves.

"I suppose I'm just like a soccer manager, passionate about my team. That's me. I do get fired up. When someone keeps knocking your best player you are

Overleaf: Upsides. The 2008 Gold Cup is a month away as Denman (Jess Allen) right, works with Kauto Star (Clifford Baker).

bound to defend him. In this form he is so good for racing. I wish I hadn't run him last time at Haydock. That was my error, but I'm chuffed for him now. I've learned from last season so he will not be running again before the Gold Cup. I realise now we need to look after him as he is best when fresh."

Denman was the one hogging the headlines early in January after a wholesale ante-post gamble on him for the John Smith's Grand National. It was a startling development given the lingering doubts about his health, and that he was still some way short of his comeback run. In a matter of days his odds plunged from 16-1 to 7-1 favourite after Nicholls hinted in his weekly *Racing Post* column that the horse would be entered for Aintree.

As you can't run if you are not in, the trainer had to make a raft of entries for races months ahead without knowing for sure that Denman's engine was as effective as it had been before treatment to his heart. Soon it was time to up the ante by putting the horse through his paces in a racecourse gallop at Wincanton late in January ahead of his much-trumpeted reappearance in the Aon Chase. After a brief moment of concern for Ruby Walsh when his mount threatened to down tools passing the racecourse stables, the signs were at the very least encouraging as they completed a circuit of the course with Neptune Collonges and Sam Thomas.

"Did I go fast enough?" asked Ruby Walsh, grinning from ear to ear.

"That's perfect, absolutely perfect, just what we wanted," purred Nicholls, who had followed the action close behind in his Range Rover. "We've had to be so patient nursing him back from a serious illness. Normally, when he comes back in like a big, fat bull, it is a question of hard graft to get the weight off him. This time we've had to build him up steadily, and by Christmas he was starting to give me the right signals."

For Paul Barber there was undeniable relief at seeing Denman come through this latest test unscathed. "After playing the fool past the stables he was really tanking down the straight towards the end, just as he normally does," he said.

So much depended on Denman's reappearance at Newbury. When it became clear that the meeting would be lost to snow, a similar race, backed by the Levy Board, was hastily put on at Kempton on the same day. This was welcomed by the Nicholls camp despite well-founded misgivings that Denman would be unsuited by the tight right-hand bends at Kempton as he has always been more effective left-handed. Beggars can't be choosers. Denman needed a run before Cheltenham. Better an outing at Kempton than no race at all.

Nicholls made no secret of his view that his champion was up against it in the Levy Board Chase after a prolonged period of idleness. "I wasn't confident because he had so much to prove. I had this nagging fear that he might not be so good again, that his hard race at Cheltenham had left its mark. The way I felt, if he did win it would be one of my finest achievements," he suggested.

Denman's comeback run ended in a shockingly comprehensive defeat in the mud at Kempton. He lost his unbeaten record over fences in a disturbing manner, jumped left-handed throughout, was unable to boss things, and was out on his feet as he trailed in twenty-three lengths behind Madison du Berlais, winner of the Hennessy that season.

In the twinkling of an eye yesterday becomes history. What matters is what we have just seen, and the latest evidence strongly indicated that the omens were not good for Denman as Cheltenham beckoned. His trainer acknowledged as much as he observed that Kauto Star was unquestionably the one to beat in the Gold Cup.

Nicholls is at his best on these occasions. It cannot have been easy for him to watch his heavyweight champion labouring so far from the finish, but he never ducks the issue when the media scrum demand instant reactions. Naturally he would have preferred time to come to terms with what had taken place, but it was never going to be possible at Kempton where he was immediately surrounded by dozens of writers, TV crews and photographers hanging on his every word.

He answered every question fully, expressed his dismay at the outcome and then admitted "Naturally I was hoping he'd whistle round here and win nicely, but it was his first run for eleven months and he didn't do badly. It's a relief to get him back on the track but it has to be possible that he reached his pinnacle in March and I wouldn't complain if he did. He may never be as good again."

Paul Barber remained upbeat. "It's great to see him back, and he will improve tons and tons for the race. It was not that bad a run and there are plenty of positives. He walked back in one piece, he wasn't pulled up and the third was a long way behind him," he said.

Bookmakers, however, were unconvinced as they slashed Kauto Star's Gold Cup odds to as short as 5-4 while easing Denman to 4-1. Paul Nicholls, for one, thought they had it about right. In the circumstances, defeat for Denman was far from a disgrace, though it soon led to his removal from the list of

Grand National entries. The decision was a straightforward one for his two owners and his trainer.

The Gold Cup was the only target for the remainder of the season, though in the run-up to the Festival there were times when Paul Nicholls again wondered if Denman would ever make it to Cheltenham. His homework improved after he was reunited most mornings with his old partner Jess Allen, back in the team after the birth of her son Jake in August. Yet one schooling session in the outdoor arena was so abysmal it left everyone present, including Paul Barber, scratching their heads.

"We were close to drawing stumps at that stage," the trainer confided at the time. It was Ruby Walsh who suggested a change of routine by popping him over a line of fences where much of the regular schooling is done in a field beside the A37. This time Denman jumped much better. Cheltenham was back on the agenda.

Even so Harry Findlay issued a warning to punters attending a Festival preview at Exeter on 26 February. Short of taking out an advertisement in the *Racing Post* he could scarcely have spelled out his fears more openly as he said, "I don't think we'll see the real Denman again even though he is in the best possible hands. Personally, knowing what I know about major sport, I don't think he's a certainty to run."

Paul Nicholls was once again the one holding all the aces in the countdown to the 2009 Gold Cup. This time he was set to field five of the sixteen runners, with the two previous winners joined by Neptune Collonges, My Will and Star de Mohaison. The one giving him all the right signals was Kauto Star, who was in the form of his life. As the big day drew near Nicholls offered an interesting insight into Kauto Star's defeat by Denman twelve months earlier.

"If I hadn't run Kauto at Ascot there might have been a different result. You might have seen a different horse at Cheltenham because I had to back off him a bit after that scare with his foot and we've had a perfect run this time after giving Ascot a miss. He had a nice easy time for a month before I started grafting the hell out of him. When you work him hard and really screw him up at home I think he is a better horse. I doubt I've ever had him better," he declared.

He also suspected that after all his trials and tribulation, Denman might need a long summer's rest before he returned to his all-conquering best. "I think he has a mountain to climb," was the phrase he used in several interviews on the eve of the Festival. Regular checks on the horse's heart continued

to be clear and he did show encouraging signs of a revival in his work in the final days before Cheltenham. Even so, Nicholls warned Denman's owners it would be little short of miraculous if he finished in the first four. This time, crucially, he told Sam Thomas not to repeat the aggressive tactics that gained the day in 2008. Instead he urged his jockey to ride with restraint, to conserve the horse's energy to help him last home.

Given the widely differing nature of the two horses' preparations their trainer has seldom, if ever, been more confident of winning a big race. He was not put off, for a moment, by the telling statistic that not a single previous winner of the Gold Cup had come back to regain his title after suffering defeat in the race. Although Nicholls is not, by nature, a gambling man, on this occasion he simply couldn't resist supporting Kauto Star with hard cash. Nor did he have an anxious moment as the horse with the almost tangible will to win justified his faith with as fine a victory in the Gold Cup as we have seen for many years.

All to play for. The field is closely packed in the early stages of the 2009 Gold Cup.

Overleaf: The crowd goes wild as Ruby Walsh celebrates Kauto Star's second victory in the Cheltenham Gold Cup in 2009.

Astonishingly Denman was the only horse that possessed the pace and courage to offer an argument, and he actually found the temerity to try to move upsides his next-door neighbour as the race came to the boil on the final bend. His monumental effort that day was an essay in resilience, but soon, inevitably, he began to struggle as lack of peak fitness told. Kauto Star, however, was strolling to his coronation. He looked like a fresh horse as he stretched clear with every ground-devouring stride, popped safely over the last and galloped on strongly all the way to the line. Although Denman was out on his feet he kept on dourly to take second place thirteen lengths behind the mighty winner.

A wave of euphoria swept over Cheltenham as Kauto Star returned in triumph. This was history on the hoof, a spectacle fit for the Queen, who was watching in person for only the second time in her reign, as Kauto Star thrillingly put an end to further argument. For the moment, at least, he was the undisputed champion. There was concern at the sight of Sam Thomas leading back Denman, but happily he wasn't lame, just exhausted after giving his all. To make a memorable day even better Nicholls once again supplied nearly all the principal players, with Neptune Collonges and My Will finishing fourth and fifth behind the gallant third Exotic Dancer.

It came at the end of a week of sustained achievement at Cheltenham that saw Nicholls and his jockey sweep the board. Walsh ended the meeting with a record seven winners, which worked out at a substantial percentage of all the races run. Nicholls set a new mark for trainers too, with five wins, and only the tantalisingly narrow defeat of Celestial Halo on the opening afternoon prevented the pair taking all four championship races.

Walsh admitted at the subsequent press conference, "Things didn't start great on Tuesday when my first ride, Kempes, stepped at the first hurdle and almost came down, my next one Tatenen fell at the third and then Celestial Halo got chinned. To win seven after that was quite something, but the one I wanted most was Kauto Star.

"I always believed in him and I hoped that the horse I believed in would turn up and show everyone else how good he is. He is the greatest I've ridden – two miles, three miles and now two Gold Cups. He is a wonderful horse."

Nicholls revealed an ambition to bring the jaunty winner back for at least two more Gold Cups, maybe three. The following morning, after a celebration dinner with a group of friends, Nicholls was back in his office at Manor Farm stables shortly after dawn. Dark rings round his eyes betrayed the nervous tension beneath the genial exterior after several nights with precious little sleep.

"I don't think I've ever been as tired as I am at the moment," he said. "I've never experienced a week like it and I was so buzzed up after the Gold Cup I spent most of the night watching replays of the race. Whatever time I go to bed I always wake up three hours later with my mind working overtime. I still can't get over the superb way Kauto Star won and the amazing comeback of Denman. After all his problems I'd say that has to be one of the performances of all time. I am proud of them both.

"I was dreading that I might end up crying my eyes out if one of them won, but I was so elated with the way Denman ran that the tears never came. The reception he got was incredible. I wasn't upset that he was beaten. Quite the opposite. The last thing anyone wanted was for anything to happen to Denman. That was my fear, though if I'd had any doubts I wouldn't have run him."

The trainer also paid a handsome tribute to his stable jockey. "My nightmare will come when Ruby is not here any more and we have to replace him. He is highly intelligent, has no fear at all and tactically he is brilliant. He is a huge asset in every way."

For Nick Child the experience of leading up the Gold Cup winner in his second season at Ditcheat was beyond price. "I've never known a feeling like it in racing and doubt I ever will again," he said as he took the horse off for his post-race dope test.

There was no question of Kauto Star running again that season, and initially Nicholls had every intention of calling a halt with Denman, too, but as he kept both horses ticking over during the next fortnight he detected a marked improvement in Denman's homework which led to a significant change of mind.

He explains "The way he was going at home I had to take him to Liverpool for the Totesport Bowl. I thought it was an ideal chance for him to go out on a winning note. He must be as tough as old boots because no horse impressed me more after Cheltenham. Given his previous problems I was astounded that he was so full of himself."

Denman's journey to Liverpool twenty days after the Gold Cup ended with the first fall of his life and briefly led to fears for his safety as screens were erected at the point of the course where he was subsequently caught after jumping the last fence riderless. Blood was flowing freely from a nasty cut on

the point of his off-fore elbow, but happily the injury was not a serious one.

Denman was led into a horse ambulance and subsequently bit Lucinda Gould on the arm while he was being treated by vets in the racecourse stables. Clearly there was still plenty of life in the patient. She recalls, "He was lame but the wound didn't require stitches. It was more a case of a dead leg, a bit like banging your funny bone against a wall, and thankfully we were able to take him home that night."

The fall came as Denman was jousting for the lead two fences out with Madison du Berlais, who was left with the race at his mercy. He was under maximum pressure from Sam Thomas at the time, took off too early at the fence, landed on it on his way down, and crashed grotesquely to the ground. No one could be sure of the outcome, though Thomas hinted that he would have won. "He'd jumped brilliantly to that point but then stepped at the fence and paid the penalty," he reported. Denman was undone on rapidly drying ground on a sharp, flat track that has always rewarded speed over stamina.

Paul Barber's overwhelming emotion was one of relief that the horse had survived relatively unscathed. "He should be right as rain in a few days. It's not too serious and with any luck he'll be back again next season. He wasn't enjoying it round here," he concluded.

Dramatic exit... Denman (Sam Thomas) turns over in the Totesport Bowl at Aintree in April 2009, as Madison du Berlais goes on to win.

It was a miserable end to a nightmare season for Denman, during which he had lost his aura of invincibility. His misfortunes left Kauto Star as the BHA's undisputed Horse of the Year at the Anglo-Irish Jump racing awards in May with an exalted rating of 186 from the BHA's head of handicapping, Phil Smith, with Denman dropping to a mark of 173. It was an accurate reflection of their last meeting at Cheltenham two months earlier. Timeform, the most reliable of professional observers, sagely concluded that Kauto Star's performance in the Gold Cup hadn't been matched or bettered in the race for forty years.

The prospect of a decider between the stable mates the following March was raised by Paul Nicholls at a party given by Clive Smith for his champion in the clubhouse at Wentworth golf course on the eve of Royal Ascot. During a long night of celebration, helped along by videos, speeches and copious amounts of champagne, tributes were paid to both horses.

Nicholls was roundly applauded as he assured the audience, "Next season my plan is to have Kauto Star and Denman in the best of health going into the Gold Cup. That will be some re-match."

CHAPTER 12

PAINFUL SEPARATION

As part of his long-term strategy to keep Kauto Star in the top flight for as long as possible Paul Nicholls decided to restrict him to only three races in 2009–10. Less, he concluded, is sometimes more. Standing high on the hill at Ditcheat early that season he shook his head in wonder at the sight of the dual Gold Cup winner stretching effortlessly towards the skyline in the early morning light.

"Kauto still loves what he does, and long may that last," he said. "He is at the stage where I don't think he can find any more improvement, but then he doesn't need to. He puts his life on the line for you every time he runs. I sometimes wonder how long this amazing rivalry between Kauto and Denman can continue. It has to have its limits, but there is no sign of a downturn yet."

The deciding showdown between the pair continued to divide opinions at all levels in racing. Nicholls conceded, "The hardest part is knowing that one of them will lose in March, though something might come along to beat the pair of them. To get them both to Cheltenham at the top of their game without any hiccups will be incredibly tough."

Although Kauto Star had won the Betfair Chase twice Nicholls was tempted to give the race a miss late in 2009 and send him instead to Down Royal, where he had been so majestic in victory twelve months earlier. Clive Smith, however, preferred a return to Haydock, not least because the Betfair Chase carried a purse of £200,000. So Haydock it was.

Naturally he was ridden by Ruby Walsh, who had long established a unique position in jump racing as a dominant force on both sides of the Irish Sea. By the end of the 2008–9 season Walsh had been champion in Ireland seven times while continuing to ride a conveyor belt of winners each season in England. Only the brilliantly gifted all-rounder Martin Molony in the years after the

Second World War could begin to match Walsh's extraordinary record of achievement. The difference for Molony was that he had to rely on a transport system that was almost Dickensian in comparison to the methods that Walsh uses today.

There has never been a jockey quite like Martin Molony. Devoutly religious, a non-smoker and non-drinker, he was equally gifted over jumps and on the flat. Short, slightly built and utterly fearless, he won the Irish 2,000 Guineas on Signal Box in 1951, finished third on the same horse in the English Derby and topped the jockeys' list in Ireland for six consecutive years from 1946 to 1951 until his all-too-brief career was cruelly cut short by a fall in September 1951 which fractured his skull. Molony, who could ride at 9st, was a major figure in England, too. In the 1949–50 season, for instance, he rode sixty-two winners over jumps in this country, a figure only surpassed by his elder brother Tim, who was champion five times in England.

Martin Molony owned a light plane in partnership with fellow jockeys Dan Moore and George Wells. It was kept in Dublin and helped reduce their travelling time to distant country meetings in Ireland. On Sunday nights he would catch the ferry from Dun Laoghaire to Liverpool, then rely on race trains and lifts from his brother in his MG. On Friday he would fly back to Dublin from Heathrow for racing in Ireland the next day.

Walsh, like Molony before him, has become adept at catching up on his sleep at airports and on planes, and in the back seats of cars as he commutes between the two countries two or three times a week. It is a punishing schedule which he continues to pursue without a word of complaint.

Heading to Haydock that November day in 2009 he shared Paul Nicholls' concerns that the speedy nature of the new chase course no longer played to Kauto Star's strengths. What neither man anticipated was that the dual Gold Cup winner would be pushed to the limit by the dashing young pretender Imperial Commander before claiming a heart-stopping triumph. The pair traded punches in the final half-mile like two heavyweights in a fight to the finish and were still locked together as they flashed past the post. If they had dug any deeper in the soggy turf they would have been tunnelling. Full marks to the Commander's jockey, Paddy Brennan, who rode over to pat Kauto Star on the neck as the two horses pulled up.

Ruby Walsh was one of many on the course who thought the challenger's final late thrust had landed a knock-out blow on the line. But the photo showed that Kauto Star had prevailed by a nose and taken his earnings close

Inseparable... The photo decides that Kauto Star has won the Betfair Chase by a nose from Imperial Commander.

to £2 million. The relief on the face of Paul Nicholls was evident as the result was announced. He leaped off the ground and punched the air with excitement before rushing off to greet the horse.

"I don't mind admitting I was more nervous today than for a long time," he reflected later. At the heart of his concern was the knowledge that for some reason his team of horses had been slower to come to hand than usual. So he anticipated that Kauto Star might get a bit tired and was thrilled to hear his jockey say afterwards that the horse had needed the race.

The mud on Walsh's face couldn't begin to disguise his delight as he declared, "This is as good a horse as we've seen and we need to start appreciating him. He is a wonderful chaser to have won twelve Grade One races. Yet they were still knocking him all through the week. It is like Manchester United. When you are on top they want to knock you. Because he has been dominant for so long people have probably not realised that he is tough, too. But he's been a battler all his life and showed it again here."

The runner-up's trainer, Nigel Twiston-Davies, was shell-shocked at the judge's verdict. "It is horrible and I can't believe it, but he has run a hell of a race. Bring on the Gold Cup," he declared with evident relish. Close study of the video suggested he had good cause to expect a different result at Cheltenham, for Imperial Commander was beginning to go clear until his mistake at the third last fence cost him vital momentum and gave Kauto Star a second chance.

Seven days later it was Denman's turn at Newbury. Paul Nicholls was not expecting fireworks. Though the horse had showed glimpses of a welcome revival he was again saddled with top weight in the Hennessy Gold Cup and an outing to Exeter for a public workout had raised more questions than it answered. "On what he showed there you wouldn't have thought he was capable of winning an egg and spoon race. I just hoped it would sharpen him up," said Nicholls. Deep down he still wondered if Denman would ever again reach the heights he had once scaled.

There was yet another unexpected twist in this tale when Denman bounced back to form with a stunning second victory under top weight in the Hennessy Gold Cup. Thirteen months earlier the big horse with the almost tangible will to win had been the subject of daily medical bulletins. Now he was the one putting his rivals under intolerable stress, though, not for the first time, he briefly threatened to decline to race, forcing Ruby Walsh to hunt him along energetically from the rear in the first half furlong to claim a position in mid division. Once he consented to put his best foot forward he proved in a different league as he served it up to his rivals before taking charge in the final mile.

A huge crowd at Newbury knew beyond doubt that they had witnessed one of those great moments in racing as they rushed to acclaim Denman after he had put a field of smart handicappers to the sword before bullying his stable companion What a Friend into submission on the run-in. It was an astonishing performance which set up the clash of the titans at Cheltenham in March with Kauto Star.

Paul Nicholls usually handles these occasions with practised ease. This time, like many others at Newbury, he was reduced to tears as he acknowledged "That has to be one of the best results we have ever had because this horse affects so many lives. Sometimes it is quite hard to watch my horses running because I become so attached to them. After all Denman's problems I had to wonder if we'd ever get him back. That is why this is a day I will never forget. To win like that after seeing off all those challenges was a monumental effort, probably his best ever run. I am so proud of him," he added.

There was a fascinating postscript when Ruby Walsh hinted that Denman was idling on the run-in and would improve markedly with the application of a pair of blinkers to help him concentrate. "He wasn't doing a tap in front," he suggested.

A month later we saw the ghost of Christmas past as Kauto Star eclipsed the record of the horse whose handsome grey statue stands sentry beside the paddock at Kempton. We were drawn to the course by the prospect of seeing the finest chaser of our times become the first to win the King George VI Chase for the fourth successive year. What we had not anticipated was that he would turn the race into a rout. Even in his swashbuckling pomp Desert Orchid, who won the King George VI Chase four times, but not consecutively, was never quite as dominant as this.

Jumping with breathtaking accuracy Kauto Star cruised up to the flanks of the long-time leader Nacarat turning for home before Ruby Walsh stole a leisurely peep over his shoulder. What he saw confirmed that the only dangers remaining were the three fences left to negotiate. Kauto Star then swept home a distance clear of Madison du Berlais, with Barbers Shop a length further back. Even those who had long admired his exceptional gifts, his work ethic and his appetite for improvement found themselves shaking their heads in wonder at this latest outpouring of his talent. It was a flawless display that brooked no argument.

Professional observers who judge these things strictly on time suggested that the winner's margin of victory could accurately be gauged at thirty-six lengths. Sometimes the pleasures of sport cannot be conveyed by mere statistics. Ruby Walsh captured the moment by tossing his gloves, goggles and finally his whip into the crowd as he came back on Kauto Star.

"You think some days he can't be as good as before but today he turned up better than ever. He is a marvellous horse, an unbelievable horse, better than ever, and possesses a cruising speed rarely seen in staying chasers. This was probably the strongest of his four King George's. They went a right gallop and good horses were struggling after a circuit, yet he never missed a beat. He was deadly," he concluded.

Conscious that history had been made, the racecourse announcer called for and received four hefty cheers and soon some of the greatest names in jump racing were queuing up to pay tribute to a horse in a million. Jonjo O'Neill, an inspired champion jockey in his time, insisted "After watching that I'd say Kauto Star is the best we'll ever see."

"... the best we'll ever see..." Ruby Walsh celebrates Kauto Star's fourth successive King George VI Chase at Kempton, December 2009 – by a magisterial thirty-six lengths from Madison du Berlais.

Beside him multiple champion Tony McCoy, who finished a distant sixth on Albertas Run, nodded in agreement. "I've only been around for fifteen years and have never seen anything like him. I've tried my best to beat him so many times but I am running out of ideas. He's got everything."

Official confirmation of what we had just witnessed came from the BHA's head of handicapping, Phil Smith, a former maths teacher who prefers to deal in figures rather than raw emotion. Pressed about the quality of this outstanding display by Kauto Star, he hinted that he had run to a figure of around 190, the highest he had ever rated the horse. Sponsors William Hill were taking no chances as they priced the winner at 6-4 to win a fifth King George in 2010.

The hype moved into overdrive in the fortnight before Denman's final race in February ahead of Cheltenham. It was fuelled by the unsurprising news that the record-breaking champion Tony McCoy would be his new jockey in the Aon Chase at Newbury and then the Gold Cup. The booking was made at the request of Barber and Findlay who wanted the best available once Ruby Walsh decided to stay loyal to Kauto Star.

Bookmakers who formed a market on the identity of Denman's new jockey found themselves running for cover as the money came for McCoy. It was supposed to be a marriage made in heaven but the champion's first ride on the giant Denman ended in painful separation at Newbury. In racing hope can be swiftly derailed, and an apparently unchallenging lap of honour for Denman in the Aon Chase turned into one of the biggest shocks for years when the champion jockey was ejected like a spent cartridge by a calamitous blunder at the third last fence. A 6-1 on chance, Denman appeared to have the race in safe keeping until he misjudged the previous fence, got in too tight, clipped the top and all but lost his hind legs on landing.

Afterwards Harry Findlay suggested with a degree of accuracy, "In less than a second he went from 100-1 on to 10-1 against."

Having somehow survived that first blunder, and surrendered the lead to Niche Market, Denman then appeared to lose his confidence, took off much too far away at the next, a ditch, and landed squarely in the fence, sending his jockey tumbling to the ground. Dress rehearsals are not meant to be like this. What happened was so unexpected that at first no one at Newbury was quite sure how to react. McCoy's ashen features betrayed his feelings as he came back clutching his whip and helmet.

Later he expressed his surprise that the chasing pack was so close when he had a peep over his shoulder turning into the straight. "I squeezed up Denman off the bend, wanting him to wing the fourth last, but I didn't get the acceleration I expected, he got in a bit tight and landed in a bit of a heap. Going to the next fence he stood off a mile too far and landed in the middle of the fence," he reported.

The champion, who has always been his worst critic, then added morosely, "There'll be a lot of people thinking that I shouldn't be riding him, and this won't have changed their minds."

Paul Nicholls took the reverse with remarkable good humour which can be explained in part by his winning the valuable race with his Grand National contender Tricky Trickster, ridden by Ruby Walsh. The trainer said, "You can see why we wanted A.P. to get to know Denman here. There was a lot of pressure on him and things didn't work out. Whatever decision you make is OK if it goes right but if it goes wrong people will knife you in the back. The main thing is that Denman is 100% after that little scare. What happened to him is a blur but no one should write him off for the Gold Cup. I wouldn't be worried about it."

Unhappy parting... Denman dumps champion jockey Tony McCoy at Newbury in February 2010.

Yet as he spoke you felt that Denman's aura had begun to evaporate a little. Harry Findlay indicated as much as he revealed, "Before today I had Denman down as a 13-8 chance for the Gold Cup. Now he's a 4-1 shot, maybe longer. That is worrying if you can count, and it is going to take a massive effort for him to beat Kauto Star."

Soon Findlay was nailing his colours firmly to Kauto Star's mast at a Cheltenham preview night in Exeter. "As a short-priced player I can say that Kauto Star has been very good to me and I will be lumping on him again. This is the first time Paul has given him only two outings ahead of the Gold Cup and I will be amazed if he doesn't run his best race."

While Denman's trainer and his owners voiced their confidence in McCoy, and confirmed that he would keep the ride at Cheltenham, others questioned his suitability for the task. It was a curious point of view when you consider that he is widely considered to be the greatest jump jockey of all time. The furious media debate that followed was in part fuelled by those lobbying for Sam Thomas to be reunited with Denman at Cheltenham. That was never going to happen.

Speaking his mind as usual shortly before the festival, Nicholls roundly condemned the criticism of McCoy before arranging for the champion to school Denman at Ditcheat ahead of the Gold Cup. "Denman can be difficult and a bit leery but saying A.P. shouldn't ride him is total rubbish. All this talk about him not suiting the horse is the biggest load of twaddle I've heard in my life. He was just unlucky at Newbury.

"It is all very well people criticising Denman and slagging off A.P. They only see them on the racecourse and haven't a clue about the horse, his mind or his character. I know him better than anybody. That day he was big and burly and sleepy. Since then he has turned inside out and improved enormously, as I expected, to the point that he is now lean and mean and tight. He's a miserable, grumpy bastard and would chase you out of his box given half a chance. Last year we were so worried about him before Cheltenham and he still finished second. He wasn't half the horse then that he is now. He's just where I want him."

At the request of Paul Barber the horse was fitted with blinkers during a routine morning's exercise late in February. He worked with enthusiasm in them but the rest of his behaviour while sporting the blinkers persuaded Nicholls not to persevere with the experiment. Nicholls felt, with some justification, that if the horse wore them at Cheltenham it might increase his chances of not starting.

With Denman nothing is straightforward, as Tony McCoy discovered when he travelled to Ditcheat to school him. After jumping a line of fences without any great enthusiasm the horse decided he had done enough for the morning. A fascinating battle of wills ensued in the next five minutes before Denman was persuaded by his rider to return to the schooling area for a second attempt. This time he jumped much better.

There were no such concerns with Kauto Star. Ruby Walsh experienced a lively ride on him as they trotted through Ditcheat with several others on the way to the schooling arena ten days before the Gold Cup. "You need your finger in the neck strap because he's as sharp as ever on the roads," he reported later to the evident amusement of the trainer.

"He nearly dropped Ruby going past the pub," laughed Nicholls. "We've found out that Kauto is lethal when he is fit and well, and I've never had him better. I do think it will take a monumental effort by Denman or anything else to beat him in his current form. It is hard to believe he is improving after all this time but to my mind his best two performances of his life came at Kempton at Christmas and in last year's Gold Cup.

"Everything comes so easily to Kauto Star, who is naturally gifted, flies along our gallop, travels easily and constantly amazes me. He is incredible. Life is a bit harder for Denman, who is such a character, so big and lazy you can't give him too much graft. His strength is his stamina, but to win any race with him you have to have him incredibly fit, which takes a bit of achieving. The great thing is that they both still want to do it as they head back to the Festival for the fifth year running. How many horses do that?" he asked.

Clifford Baker, too, seemed to be leaning towards Kauto Star. "The aggressive streak he's shown lately is a good sign," he suggested. "When he is nearing top form he tries to bite his galloping companion, Big Bucks, and he also had a nip at Denman when they were having their picture taken recently. He's definitely ready."

CHAPTER 13

THE SKY FELL IN

It seemed as if the entire sporting world tuned in for the ultimate showdown at Cheltenham on Friday 19 March, which just happened to be Kauto Star's tenth birthday. That was the most obvious story line on a day when history beckoned, but in racing the result rarely matches the narrative.

Rain had been falling steadily for almost two hours by the time the runners appeared in the paddock for the Gold Cup. You could almost reach out and touch the tension as stern-faced riders were legged into the saddle. This was not a time for light-hearted banter for there is a dark side to jump racing that is never far from the surface and the apprehension runs deepest when so much is at stake. The shadow of the next fall makes for a humility among jockeys that is unknown in less demanding sports. For the horses the risks are even greater. The unspoken fear as the field of eleven was sent off by the starter was that one of them might not return.

For Kauto Star's legion of supporters hoping he could deliver the best birthday present of all it was disturbing to see his old jumping frailties return as early as the eighth fence where he ploughed perilously through the birch, tipped onto his nose and was almost down. Displaying an instinct born of survival, Ruby Walsh somehow defied gravity by remaining in the saddle. Yet in that instant Kauto Star's chance of a third Gold Cup had all but gone for it seemed to knock the stuffing out of him. Until then he had been gliding through the race with nonchalant ease, but from that point he was struggling to find sufficient wind in his sails.

"After that mistake I was fighting a lost cause. I couldn't get him on an even keel or properly balanced," Ruby Walsh confirmed later.

Out in front Carruthers had been taking them along at a searching pace, closely attended by Denman, Imperial Commander and Cooldine, with Kauto

Team mates... (left) Kauto Star and Denman nose to nose before the start of the 2010 Cheltenham Gold Cup and below, racing side by side.

The race comes to the boil. Denman (centre) is well placed between Carruthers (right) and Imperial Commander (left) with Kauto Star (noseband) mid air.

The crowd reacts in dismay (and one woman can't even bear to watch) as Kauto Star falls heavily four out.

Imperial Commander surges ahead of Denman after the last fence to win the Cheltenham Gold Cup by seven lengths.

Star hanging on grimly after his untimely blunder without really offering much hope of a revival. Going out into the country for the last time he was still in there pitching, just behind the leaders, like a wounded boxer desperately clinging on as he waited for his head to clear. The pace was unrelenting, yet at the fence at the top of the hill, five out, the favourite threw in a mighty leap which took him onto the heels of the leaders and briefly gave his backers renewed belief that he wouldn't be giving up his title lightly.

Then the sky fell in. Kauto Star barely rose at the next fence and took as bad a fall as you will ever see at Cheltenham. Time seemed to stand still as he pitched horrifyingly onto his head, turned over, then slithered along the ground some way behind his jockey. It was the type of fall which can kill or maim and reminded us of all the concerns that surrounded the horse when he used to ignore his fences in his impetuous youth. There was a huge roar of relief from the stands when he scrambled to his feet and was swiftly caught by Walsh. The champ had survived a knock-out blow. Hopefully he would be back.

With Kauto Star abruptly removed from the script the closing stages of the 2010 Gold Cup swiftly developed into a head-to-head encounter between Denman and Imperial Commander. Tony McCoy was the first to play his cards as he pushed his partner into a narrow lead running down the hill for the last time. The response was immediate as Denman willingly pounded forward, but just behind Paddy Brennan was stalking him with stealthy intent on Imperial Commander.

Rounding the final bend the pair were level. This wasn't quite the duel we had anticipated but it was undeniably compelling as they turned for home

with all guns blazing. Could the stout-hearted grinder find more in the closing stages or would the fleet-footed challenger see him off on the final, unforgiving hill? We soon had the answer.

Destiny was calling for Imperial Commander, who showed ahead for the first time landing over the second last and gradually began to stretch clear. He was not for stopping and galloped on relentlessly to take the prize by seven lengths, with the 2009 Grand National winner Mon Mome snatching third place from Carruthers in the last stride.

Paul Nicholls was one of the first to congratulate Paddy Brennan as he made his way on Imperial Commander through the cheering crowds towards the winner's enclosure. The jubilant jockey had learned his trade with him when he first moved to England. Moments later Nigel Twiston-Davies could be forgiven for telling Channel 4 "Kauto Star and Denman. That's all I've heard for the past three months. I know they've been good for racing but this wasn't ever a two-horse race. We were always going to bloody win it!"

"... he's all right, I'm all right..." Ruby Walsh canters Kauto Star back after their fall.

The sight of Ruby Walsh cantering back on Kauto Star was the happiest of the week. He reported "Kauto Star was up after the fall before me. He was going by me and I jumped up and caught him. It is always a relief when a good horse like him gets up and is OK. He is all right, I am all right and there will be another day. There is not a bother on him but it would have been the worst day if he wasn't all right," he reflected, echoing the thoughts of those watching at Cheltenham or on TV.

Paul Nicholls accurately described Kauto Star's initial blunder as baffling and his second as unprintable. "He's got away with a few bad mistakes in his career and I suppose he was always going to do it one day. It's such a shame he did it here because I've no doubt he was in the best shape he's ever been in. That's racing.

"I was proud of Denman, who again covered himself with glory though he may just have lost a little bit of speed. In this sport there is no such thing as a two-horse race. Good luck to Imperial Commander. He did everything right. There is always a changing of the guard."

Tony McCoy, the ultimate competitor, couldn't disguise his dismay at failing to land the Gold Cup on Denman. "Second is better than third, and better than where Ruby ended up," he conceded. "You think Kauto Star is the only horse that will beat you but when he is out of the race and something else does it is disappointing."

Kauto Star's painful departure effectively put an end to further debate on comparisons with the mighty Arkle, whose memory is secure in the mists of time. Even the most ardent lobbyists for their fallen hero can no longer claim that his record bears comparison with the horse who won the Gold Cup three years running between 1964 and 1966 and was head and shoulders above his contemporaries before his career was ended prematurely by injury.

While there is no denying the magnifying effects of nostalgia it is legitimate to recall that Arkle's most memorable feats included routinely demolishing fields of decent handicappers to whom he was required to concede lumps of weight. No one should question Kauto Star's claims to greatness, but most of us would readily settle for an acknowledgement that he is the best chaser since Arkle. It is no more than he deserves.

The headlines in the days after the Gold Cup rightly heralded the arrival of a new champion and lauded his tousle-haired trainer who hosted a marathon party at his local, the Hollow Bottom in Naunton, snatched a few hours sleep

Not how the script was written... Tony McCoy cannot disguise his disappointment.

179

and was back at the pub the next morning to parade Imperial Commander. Naturally Twiston-Davies was wearing his familiar ancient duffel coat that would not be out of place on the Antiques Roadshow. The Gold Cup was the Commander's sixth triumph at Cheltenham. No wonder his trainer was frustrated that his horse was ignored in all the pre-race ballyhoo.

Much later Paul Nicholls would talk of a sense of guilt, of a feeling that he had let people down at Cheltenham. It was, of course, nonsense because, in racing, past performance is not necessarily a guarantee of future success, particularly at the seething cauldron of the Festival. Yet his words gave an intriguing insight into the forces that continue to drive him on to be the best in his business.

Time would not diminish his savage disappointment at seeing Kauto Star crash dramatically out of his fourth Gold Cup. The horse was also feeling sorry for himself in the days after his heavy fall. At first his neck was so sore that he could not reach down to his manger on the floor. Clifford Baker solved the problem by placing his manger on a base of three tyres.

Denman's subsequent extraordinary performance in finishing fourth in the Guinness Gold Cup at Punchestown, despite hanging so badly left he almost ran off the track, was another unexpected reverse for the trainer who immediately blamed himself for running the horse on a right-handed track.

The beauty of horse racing is that for trainers, owners, jockeys and punters there is always another day, another race, a fresh challenge, and long before Nicholls' two Gold Cup winners were turned out to grass for their annual summer break he had already chosen the key prizes to target at the end of the year.

"It would be great if Denman could win a record third Hennessy, though it is going to be seriously difficult for him to do it off a handicap mark of 182, so I might take him straight to the Lexus Chase in Ireland. And if Kauto Star can add a fifth King George it would mean the world to me," he suggested late in April as the flat season took centre stage once more. Further ahead, he is already anticipating another double-handed assault on the Gold Cup. History will be against the pair triumphing again at the Festival, for time moves on and both will be in the veteran stage when they return to Cheltenham next March at the age of eleven.

Yet normal rules have never applied to Kauto Star and Denman and there could yet be another twist in their uplifting story. Watching them in action once more will be something to brighten the winter.

Normal rules don't apply... Paul Nicholls with Kauto Star and Denman at Ditcheat 2010.

STATISTICS

Kauto Star		Denman
19.03.2000	**Date of Birth**	17.04.2000
France	**Place of Birth**	Eire
Marie-Louise Aubert	**Breeder**	Colman O'Flynn
Village Star (FR)	**Sire**	Presenting
Kauto Relka (FR)	**Dam**	Polly Puttens
Bay	**Colour**	Chestnut
Clive Smith	**Owner**	Paul Barber and Maggie Findlay
Paul Nicholls	**Trainer**	Paul Nicholls
Nick Child	**Lad/Lass**	Lucinda Gould
16 hands 2	**Height**	17 hands
520 kilos	**Racing Weight**	555 kilos
190	**BHA rating**	182
	Point to Points	1
34	**Races**	21
20	**Wins**	15
13	**Grade 1 Wins**	4
3	**Falls**	1
1	**Unseated rider**	1
£2,012,654	**Total Prize Money**	£1,011,650

Kauto Star's Racing Record

2003

Bordeaux Le Bouscat – 1st March
2,900m Hurdle, 5,760 Euros

1 Star Glory	3-65	C Pieux
2 Kauto Star	3-65	F Barrao
3 Nagging	3-65	J Ricou

Short Head, 2 ½ lengths

Kauto Star beat Star Glory but the result was reversed on appeal.

Enghein – 14th April 3,000m Hurdle, 17,280 Euros

1 Kauto Star	3-64	F Barrao
2 Robin De Nonant	3-64	B Gicquel
3 Ruben Bravo	3-66	L Metais

5 lengths, 6

Auteuil – 4th May 3,000m Hurdle 19,200 Euros

1 Kauto Star	3-65	F Barrao
2 Fighter Cat	3-62	J Marion
3 Martin Pecheur	3-63	A Kondrat

Head, 5 lengths

Auteuil – 27th September 3,600m Hurdle, 31,200 Euros

1 Kauto Star	3-65	J Guiheneuf
2 Il Manifico	3-66	C Pieux
3 Fighter Cat	3-65	P Chevalier

3/4 length, 6

Auteuil – 11th October 3,600m Hurdle, 56,250 Euros, Grade 2

1 Maia Eria	3-62	M Delmares
2 Mesange Royale	3-64	A Kondrat
3 Il Manifico	3-66	F Barrao

6 lengths, 1 ½ Kauto Star (J Guiheneuf) Fell

Auteuil – 2nd November 3,600m Hurdle, 94,500 Euros Grade 2

1 Maia Eria	3-63	C Pieux
2 Kauto Star	3-65	J Guiheneuf
3 Il Manifico	3-65	F Barrao

10 lengths, 6

2004

Auteuil – 7th March
3,600m Hurdle, 54,000 Euros Grade 2

1 River Charm	4-65	P Marsac
2 Maia Eria	4-66	C Pieux
3 Kauto Star	4-68	J Guiheneuf

6 lengths, 4

Auteuil – 27th March 3,600m Hurdle, 54,000 Euros Grade 3

1 Maia Eria	4-66	C Pieux
2 Riiver Charm	4-67	P Marsac
3 Kizit Lo	4-65	C Santerne

15 lengths, 2 ½

Kauto Star (J Guiheneuf) fifth

Auteuil – 24th April 3,900m Hurdle, 67,500 Euros Grade 2

1 Maia Eria	4-66	C Pieux
2 Mondul	4-65	O McPhail
3 Kauto Star	4-66	J Guiheneuf

15 lengths, 4

Auteuil – 30th May 3,900m Hurdle, 54,000 Euros Grade 3

1 Kauto Star	4-65	J Guiheneuf
2 River Charm	4-66	P Marsac
3 Mondul	4-65	O McPhail

8 lengths, 1 ½

2004-05

Newbury – 29th December 2m 2½f Nov Chase £8,840
1 Kauto Star	4-10-7	R Walsh 2-1 Jt Fav
2 Foreman	6-11-4	AP McCoy
3 Sleep Bai	5-11-4	M Fitzgerald
9 lengths, 15

Exeter – 31st January 2m 1½f Nov Chase £9,288
1 Mistral De La Cour	5-11-0	A Thornton 20-1
2 Kauto Star	5-11-4	R Walsh
Short head

2005-06

Exeter – 1st November 2m 1½f Chase, Limited
Handicap Grade 2 £37,063
1 Monkerhostin	8-10-5	R Johnson 10-1
2 Kauto Star	5-10-9	R Walsh
3 Ashley Brook	7-11-4	P Brennan
4 lengths, 9

Sandown – 3rd December 2m Chase Grade 1 £71,275
1 Kauto Star	5-11-7	M Fitzgerald 5-2 Jt Fav
2 Ashley Brook	7-11-7	AP McCoy
3 Oneway	8-11-7	G Lee
1½ lengths, 8.

Cheltenham – 15th March 2m Chase Grade 1 £165,358
1 Newmill	8-11-10	A McNamara 16-1
2 Fota Island	10-11-10	AP McCoy
3 Mister McGoldrick	9-11-10	D Elsworth
9 lengths, 1 1/2.
Kauto Star (R Walsh) Fell

2006-2007

Aintree – 22nd October 2m 4f Chase Grade 2 £28,510
1 Kauto Star	6-11-10	R Walsh Evens Fav
2 Armaturk	9-11-1	J Maguire
3 Inca Trail	10-10-4	G Lee
21 lengths, 8

Haydock – 18th November 3m Chase Grade 1 £114,040
1 Kauto Star	6-11-8	R Walsh 11-10 Fav
2 Beef Or Salmon	10-11-8	A McNamara
3 L'Ami	7-11-8	AP McCoy
17 lengths, 1

Sandown – 2nd December 2m Chase. Grade 1 £79,828
1 Kauto Star	6-11-7	R Walsh 4-9 Fav
2 Voy Por Ustedes	5-11-7	R Thornton
3 Oneway	9-11-7	R Johnson
7 lengths, 7.

Kempton – 26th December 3m Chase. Grade 1 £114,040
1 Kauto Star	6-11-10	R Walsh 8-13 Fav
2 Exotic Dancer	6-11-10	AP McCoy
3 Racing Demon	6-11-10	G Lee
8 lengths, 1 1/4

Newbury – 10th February 3m Chase Grade 2 £28,510
1 Kauto Star	7-11-10	R Walsh 2-9 Fav
2 L'Ami	8-11-0	AP McCoy
3 Royal Auclair	10-11-6	L Heard
Neck, 14 lengths

Cheltenham – 16th March 3m 2½f Chase. Grade 1
£242,335
1 Kauto Star	7-11-10	R Walsh 5-4 Fav
2 Exotic Dancer	7-11-10	AP McCoy
3 Turpin Green	8-11-10	A Dobbin
2½ lengths, 2½

2007-08

Aintree – 28th October 2m 4f Chase Grade 2 £29,400
1 Monet's Garden	9-10-10	A Dobbin 9-4 Fav
2 Kauto Star	7-11-10	R Walsh
3 Exotic Dancer	7-11-3	AP McCoy
1½ lengths, 20

Haydock – 24th November 3m Chase. Grade 1 £114,040
1 Kauto Star	7-11-7	S Thomas 4-5 Fav
2 Exotic Dancer	7-11-7	B Geraghty
3 Beef or Salmon	11-11-7	D O'Regan
½ length, 18

Kempton – 26th December 3m Chase Grade 1 £126,033

1 Kauto Star	7-11-10	R Walsh 4-6 Fav
2 Our Vic	9-11-10	T Murphy
3 Exotic Dancer	7-11-10	AP McCoy

11 lengths, 1¼

Ascot – 16th February 2m 5 ½f Chase Grade 1 £84,510

1 Kauto Star	8-11-7	R Walsh 4-11 Fav
2 Monet's Garden	10-11-7	A Dobbin
3 Racing Demon	8-11-7	P Molony

8 lengths, neck

Cheltenham – 14th March 3m 2 ½ f Chase Grade 1 £268,279

1 Denman	8-11-10	S Thomas 9-4
2 Kauto Star	8-11-10	R Walsh
3 Neptune Collonges	7-11-10	M Fitzgerald

7 lengths, short head

Aintree – 3rd April 3m 1f Chase Grade 1 £91,216

1 Our Vic	10-11-10	T Murphy 9-1
2 Kauto Star	8-11-10	R Walsh
3 Exotic Dancer	8-11-10	AP McCoy

Nose, 14 lengths

2008-09

Down Royal – 1st November 3m Chase. Grade 1 £65,882

1 Kauto Star	8-11-10	R Walsh 2-5 Fav
2 Light On The Broom	12-11-10	M Walsh
3 Knight Legend	9-11-10	A Leigh

11 lengths, 11

Haydock – 22nd November 3m Chase Grad 1 £127, 341

1 Snoopy Loopy	10-11-7	S Durack 33-1
2 Tamarinbleu	8-11-7	T O'Brien
3 Exotic Dancer	8-11-7	AP McCoy

½ length, 2 1/4

Kauto Star (S Thomas) Unseated Rider

Kempton – 26th December 3m Chase Grade 1, £130,864

1 Kauto Star	8-11-10	R Walsh 10-11 Fav
2 Albertas Run	7-11-10	AP McCoy
3 Voy Por Ustedes	7-11-10	R Thornton

8 lengths, ½

Cheltenham – 13th March 3m 2½f Chase Grade 1, £270,797

1 Kauto Star	9-11-10	R Walsh 7-4 Fav
2 Denman	9-11-10	S Thomas
3 Exotic Dancer	9-11-10	AP McCoy

13 lengths, 2½

2009-2010

Haydock – 21st November 3m Chase. Grade 1. £112,660

1 Kauto Star	9-11-7	R Walsh 4-6 Fav
2 Imperial Commander	8-11-7	P Brennan
3 Madison du Berlais	8-11-7	T Scudamore

Nose, 24 lengths

Kempton – 26th December 3m Chase Grade 1, 114,020

1 Kauto Star	9-11-10	R Walsh 8-13 Fav
2 Madison du Berlais	8-11-10	T Scudamore
3 Barbers Shop	7-11-10	B Geraghty

36 lengths, 1

Cheltenham – 19th March 3m 2½f Chase Grade 1, £270,797

1 Imperial Commander	9-11-10	P Brennan 7-1
2 Denman	10-11-10	AP McCoy
3 Mon Mome	10-11-10	A Coleman

7 lengths, 23

Kauto Star (R Walsh) Fell

Denman's Racing Record

2005

Liscarrol – 20th March Maiden Div 2

1. Denman   C Sweeney 6-4f
2. Just Naturally   M O'Coonor
3. Snow Term   J Sheehan
8 lengths, ¾

2005-2006

Wincanton – 23rd October 2m 6f Novices' Hurdle

1 Denman	5-10-11	C Williams 5-6f
2 Lyes Green	4-10-11	L Aspell
3 Alphabetical	6-10-11	N Fehilly

1¼ lengths, 14

Wincanton – 17th November 2m 6f Novices' Hurdle
£5,009

1 Denman	5-11-4	C Williams 2-1
2 Karanja	6-10-12	A Thornton
3 Surface To Air	4-10-9	R Young

16 lengths, 2½

Wincanton – 17th November 2m 6f Novices' Hurdle
£5,009

1 Denman	5-11-4	C Williams 2-1
2 Karanja	6-10-12	A Thornton
3 Surface To Air	4-10-9	R Young

16 lengths, 2½

Cheltenham – 1st January 2m 4½ f Novices Hurdle
£22,808 Grade 1

1 Denman	6-11-7	R Walsh 5-2
2 The Cool Guy	6-11-7	C Llewellyn
3 Boychuk	5-11-7	R Johnson

21 lengths, ¾

Bangor-on-Dee – 10th February 3m Novices' Hurdle
£6,381

1 Denman	6-11-13	C Williams 1-12
2 One Sniff	7-11-5	A Dobbin
3 Abraham Smith	6-11-10	M Nicholls

17 lengths, 16

Cheltenham – 15th March 2m 5f Novices' Hurdle
£57,020 Grade 1

1 Nicanor	5-11-7	P Carberry 17-2
2 Denman	6-11-7	R Walsh
3 Refinement	7-11-0	AP McCoy

2½ lengths, 6

2006-07

Exeter – 31st October 2m 1½f Novices' Chase £10,409

1 Denman	6-10-12	R Walsh 1-3
2 Penzance	5-11-4	R Thornton
3 Keepthedreamalive	8-10-9	D Jacob

10 lengths, 5

Cheltenham – 1st November 2m 4½f Novices' Chase
£12,526

1 Denman	6-11-4	R Walsh 4-6
2 Don't Push It	6-11-4	AP McCoy
3 Il Duce	6-11-4	R Thornton

¾ length, 17

Newbury – 26th November 2m 4f Novices' Chase £19, 957

1 Denman	6-11-7	S Thomas 2-11
2 Snakebite	6-11-0	N Fehilly
3 High Chimes	7-11-0	P Molony

12 lengths, 52

Newbury – 10th February 3m Novices' Chase £11,710

1 Denman	7-11-12	R Walsh 1-3
2 Mr Pointment	8-11-9	AP McCoy
3 Standin Obligation	8-11-12	T Murphy

36 lengths, 93

Cheltenham – 14th March 3m 1/2f Novices Chase
£96,934 Grade 1

1 Denman	7-11-4	R Walsh 6-5
2 Snowy Morning	7-11-4	M Fitzgerald
3 According To John	7-11-4	A Dobbin

10 lengths, 3½

2007-08

Newbury – 1st December 3m 2½f Hcp Chase £85,530
Grade 3

1 Denman	7-11-12	S Thomas 5-1
2 Dream Alliance	6-10-7	J Moore
3 Character Building	7-10-0	D O'Regan

11 lengths, 8

Leopardstown – 28th December 3m Chase £83,783
Grade 1

1 Denman	7-11-10	R Walsh
2 Mossbank	7-11-10	D Russell
3 The Listener	8-11-10	D Jacob

4 lengths, head

Newbury – 9th February 3m Chase £28,510 Grade 2

1 Denman	8-11-10	S Thomas 1-4f
2 Regal Heights	7-11-4	R Walsh
3 Celestial Gold	10-11-0	T Murphy

20 lengths, 9

Cheltenham – 14th March 3m 2½ f Chase £268,279
Grade 1

1 Denman	8-11-10	S.Thomas 9-4
2 Kauto Star	8-11-10	R Walsh
3 Neptune Collonges	7-11-10	M Fitzgerald

7 lengths, sh head

2008-09

Kempton – 7th February 3m Chase £30,215 Grade 2

1 Madison du Berlais	8-11-6	T Scudamore 12-1
2 Denman	9-11-10	R Walsh
3 Albertas Run	8-11-5	AP McCoy

23 lengths, 25

Cheltenham – 13th March 3m 2½ f Chase £270,797
Grade 1

1 Kauto Star	9-11-10	R Walsh 7-4
2 Denman	9-11-10	S Thomas
3 Exotic Dancer	9-11-10	AP McCoy

13 lengths, 2½

Aintree – 2nd April 3m 1f Chase £91,216 Grade 2

1 Madison du Berlais	8-11-10	T.Scudamore 12-1
2 Exotic Dancer	9-11-10	AP McCoy
3 Albertas Run	8-11-5	R Thornton

Denman (S Thomas) Fell
4½ lengths, 17

2009-10

Newbury – 28th November 3m, 2½f Hacp Chase £114,020
Grade 3

1 Denman	9-11-12	R Walsh 11-4
2 What A Friend	6-10-4	S Thomas
3 Niche Market	8-9-11	A Glassonbury

3½ lengths, 3 3/4

Newbury – 13th February 3m Chase £28,639 Grade 2

1 Tricky Trickster	7-11-3	R Walsh
2 Niche Market	9-11-6	A Glassonbury
3 Air Force One	8-11-10	P Molony

Denman (AP McCoy) Unseated Rider
Sh Head, 18

Cheltenham – 19th March 3m 2½f Chase £270,797
Grade 1

1 Imperial Commander	9-11-10	P Brennan 7-1
2 Denman	10-11-10	AP McCoy
3 Mon Mome	10-11-10	A Coleman

7 lengths, 23

Punchestown – 21st April 3m, 1f Chase £119,469
Grade 1

1 Planet Of Sound	8-11-10	R Johnson 14-1
2 War Of Attrition	11-11-10	D Russell
3 Cooldine	8-11-10	P Townend

Denman (AP McCoy) 4th

KAUTO STAR - Pedigree

VILLAGE STAR (FR) ch. 1983	MOULIN (GB) ch. 1976	MILL REEF (USA) b. 1968 [CS
		HIGH FIDELYTY (FR) 1968
	GLITTER (FR) dkb/br. 1976	RELIANCE (FR) ch. 1962 [SP]
		GLISTENING (GB) br. 1968
KAUTO RELKA (FR) b. 1991	PORT ETIENNE (FR) b. 1983	MILL REEF (USA) b. 1968 [CS]
		SIERRA MORENA (ITY) ch. 1973
	KAUTORETTE (FR) dkb/br. 1981	KAUTOKEINO (FR) b. 1967
		VERDURETTE (FR) ch. 1971

NEVER BEND (USA) b. 1960 [BI]	**NASRULLAH** (GB) b. 1940 [B]
	LALUN (USA) b. 1952 *
MILAN MILL (USA)* b. 1962	**PRINCEQUILLO** (IRE) b. 1940 [IS]
	VIRGINIA WATER (USA) gr/r. 1953
HAUTAIN (FR) ch. 1957	**SKY HIGH** (GB) br. 1943
	HAURA (FR) ch. 1946
PALADRINA (GER) blk/br. 1962	**ORSINI** (GER) blk. 1954
	PROMPT PAYMENT (GB) br. 1950 *
TANTIEME (FR) b. 1947 [S]	**DEUX-POUR-CENT** (FR) b. 1941
	TERKA (FR) br. 1942
RELANCE (FR)* ch. 1952	**RELIC** (USA) blk. 1945
	POLAIRE (FR) b. 1947
AUREOLE (GB) ch. 1950 [C]	**HYPERION** (GB) ch. 1930 [BC]
	ANGELOLA (GB) b. 1945 *
CAUSERIE (GB) b. 1961	**CAGIRE** (FR) br. 1947
	HAPPY THOUGHT (GB) b. 1953
NEVER BEND (USA) b. 1960 [BI]	**NASRULLAH** (GB) b. 1940 [B]
	LALUN (USA) b. 1952 *
MILAN MILL (USA)* b. 1962	**PRINCEQUILLO** (IRE) b. 1940 [IS]
	VIRGINIA WATER (USA) gr/r. 1953
CANISBAY (GB) ch. 1961	**DOUTELLE** (GB) ch. 1954
	STROMA (GB) ch. 1955
SAIGON (ITY) ch. 1965	**MOSSBOROUGH** (GB) ch. 1947 [C]
	SAVONA (GB) ch. 1959
RELKO (GB) blk/br. 1960 [S]	**TANERKO** (FR) b. 1953
	RELANCE (FR) ch. 1952 *
CRANBERRY (GB) b. 1957	**AUREOLE** (GB) ch. 1950 [C]
	BIG BERRY (GB) b. 1951
LIONEL (FR) ch. 1963	**HERBAGER** (FR) b. 1956 [CS]
	LA STRADA (FR) b. 1955
TYROLINA (FR) ch. 1964	**TYRONE** (FR) b. 1954
	CATALICA (FR) ch. 1957

DENMAN - Pedigree

PRESENTING (GB) br. 1992	**MTOTO** (GB) b. 1983	**BUSTED** (GB) b. 1963 [S]
		AMAZER (FR) b. 1967
	PD'AZY (IRE) b. 1984	**PERSIAN BOLD** (IRE) br. 1975
		BELLE VIKING (FR) ch. 1976
POLLY PUTTENS (GB) b. 1982	**POLLERTON** (GB) b. 1974	**RARITY** (GB) b. 1967
		NILIE (GB) b. 1968
	MY PUTTENS (IRE) 1972	**DAVID JACK** (GB) b. 1963
		RAILSTOWN (GB) 1965

CREPELLO (GB) ch. 1954 [P]	**DONATELLO** (FR) ch. 1934 [P]	
	CREPUSCULE (GB) ch. 1948	
SANS LE SOU (GB) b. 1957	**VIMY** (FR) b. 1952	
	MARTIAL LOAN (GB) gr. 1950	
MINCIO (FR) b. 1957	**RELIC** (USA) blk. 1945	
	MERISE (FR) b. 1945	
ALZARA (GB) ch. 1961	**ALYCIDON** (GB) ch. 1945 [P]	
	ZABARA (GB) ch. 1949	
BOLD LAD (IRE) b. 1964	**BOLD RULER** (USA) br. 1954 [BI]	
	BARN PRIDE (IRE) ch. 1957	
RELKARUNNER (GB) b. 1968	**RELKO** GB) blk/br. 1960 [S]	
	RUNNING BLUE (GB) ch. 1957	
RIVERMAN (USA) br. 1969 [IC]	**NEVER BEND** (USA) b. 1960 [BI]	
	RIVER LADY (USA) b. 1963	
VALLARTA (FR) ch. 1966	**SHESHOON** (GB) ch. 1956	
	VALE (FR) ch. 1959	
HETHERSETT (GB) b. 1959	**HUGH LUPUS** (FR) b. 1952	
	BRIDE ELECT (GB) b. 1952	
WHO CAN TELL (GB) ch. 1958	**WORDEN** (FR) ch. 1949 [S]	
	JAVOTTE (USA) ch. 1948	
RELKO (GB) blk/br. 1960 [S]	**TANERKO** (FR) b. 1953	
	RELANCE (FR) ch. 1952 *	
ARCTIC MELODY (GB) ch. 1962	**ARCTIC SLAVE** (IRE) b. 1950	
	BELL BIRD (GB) ch. 1954	
PAMPERED KING (GB) b. 1954	**PRINCE CHEVALIER** (FR) b. 1943 [C]	
	NETHERTON MAID (GB) b. 1944	
JUDY OWENS (GB) ch. 1957	**OWENSTOWN** (GB) gr. 1934	
	RED TAPE (IRE) br. 1946	
ESCART (FR) ch. 1955	**TURMOIL** (FR) b. 1945	
	ESCALADE (FR) 1948	
U (GB) b. 1956	**CACADOR** (GB) 1935	
	CARAGANA 1946	

PICTURE CREDITS